61ST BATTERY, CANADIAN FIELD ARTILLERY.

THE DIARY

OF THE

61st BATTERY

CANADIAN FIELD ARTILLERY

FOREWORD.

In the following pages will be found a partial record of the daily activities of the 61st Battery, Canadian Field Artillery, during the War. It was written from day to day under circumstances and conditions of a widely varying kind; but all these circumstances and conditions had this in common that they demanded brevity and offered every discouragement to literary excellence.

Accordingly, no attempt has been made to produce anything more than a rough framework upon which each man of our Battery may hang his own experiences. Doubtless each man will render this framework vital and even splendid by the multitudes of memories which the bare and simple entries will call forth.

The record is published primarily for the men of the Battery and their friends; and in order that each man's personal experiences may be entered, the publishers have been asked to leave a few blank lines at the end of each day's entry. Nominal Rolls, showing the members of the Battery at various periods, have been added.

Those who are not members of the Battery, and who may chance to read this record, may wonder why so little mention has been made of individuals. This has been the case not because acts of courage or gallantry or instances of devotion to duty have been few, but because they have been matters of daily occurrence, and because the men of the Battery, without exception, "carried on" under conditions which constantly demanded true soldierly qualities.

With this brief introduction, therefore, our autobiography issues forth—defects and all.

CONTENTS.

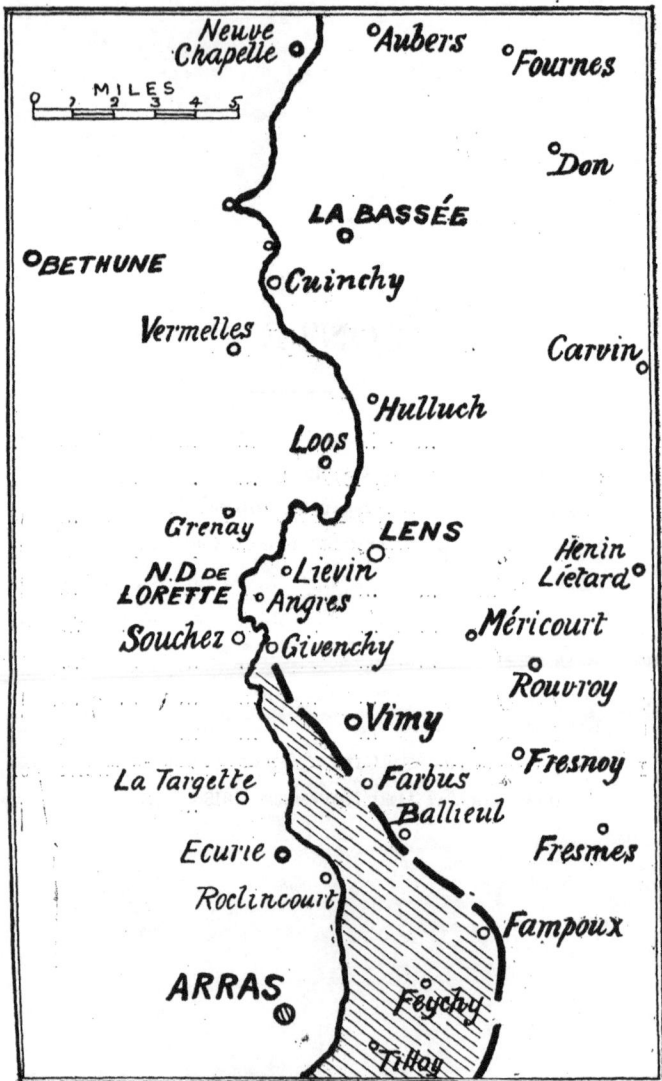

THE FRONT FROM LA BASSÉE TO ARRAS IN 1917.

SKETCH OF MOBILIZATION AND PERIOD OF TRAINING.

OFFICE opened for recruiting of the 61st Overseas Battery Canadian Field Artillery on 3rd April, 1916, at the Hull Block, Lethbridge, Alberta. The following officers were provisionally appointed :—

Lieut. Virtue, A. G.
Lieut. Oliver, A. G.
Lieut. Raley, G. S.

1916.
4th MAY.—Moved into Henderson Park Barracks.

21st MAY.—Captain C. H. Collinson took over command of the Battery.

28th MAY.—12.30 a.m.—Battery entrained for Petawawa Camp, Ontario. Men fell in at 11 p.m., 27th May, in front of *Herald* Office, and, the Roll being called, all were reported present.

28th MAY.—Muster Roll Call and Route March at Moose Jaw.

29th MAY.—Route March at Winnipeg.

30th MAY.—Route March at Fort William.

31st MAY.—Route March at North Bay.

1st JUNE.—Arrived at Petawawa Camp at 4 a.m.

14th JUNE—Lieut. R. H. Babbage attached as supernumerary.

26th JUNE.—Inspected by His Royal Highness The Duke of Connaught on Drury Plain.

1916.

25th JULY.—Inspected by General Gwatkin.

4th AUGUST.—Lieut. R. H. Babbage transferred to Brigade Headquarters.

8th SEPTEMBER.—7.30 p.m.—Battery entrained at Petawawa.

10th SEPTEMBER.—6 p.m.—Arrived at Halifax.

11th SEPTEMBER.—11 a.m.—Marched on to troopship. It is the R.M.S. *Cameronia*, afterwards sunk while in use as a transport.

13th SEPTEMBER.—6 a.m.—The *Cameronia*, with the Twelfth and Fifteenth Artillery Brigades on board, steamed out of Halifax. The line of transports was as follows :— H.M. Cruiser *Drake*, Transports *Northland*, *Scandinavian*, *Cameronia*, *Metagama*.

21st SEPTEMBER.—About 2 p.m. on 21st September our fleet of four transports and H.M.S. *Drake* was joined by a flotilla of five torpedo boat destroyers. The transports steamed up and speeded for port independently. Destroyer No. 74 stayed by our transport (the *Cameronia*) until we reached Liverpool at 4 p.m. on 22nd September. We disembarked at 5 p.m. and entrained at 6 p.m.

23rd SEPTEMBER.—Arrived at Milford Station (Surrey) at 4 a.m., and marched into Witley Camp Artillery Lines at 5 a.m.

1917.

22nd JANUARY.—Lieut. C. H. Locke and the Right Section of 59th Battery C.F.A. (Winnipeg) were taken on strength of the Battery, as the new Establishment for a Field Artillery Battery provides for six guns and about 195 men.

Shortly after this date Major G. S. Browne, who had seen service in France as a Captain, took over command of the new 6-gun Battery, Captain Collinson remaining as Captain.

NOMINAL ROLL.

Officers and Other Ranks of 61st BATTERY, C.F.A., at date of leaving England for France.

Major Browne, G. S.
Captain Collinson, C. H.
Lieut. Locke, C. H.
Lieut. Virtue, A. G.
Lieut. Oliver, A. G.
Lieut. Raley, G. S.
Lieut. Babbage, R. H.
327960 Dvr. Allen, R.
331903 Gnr. Armstrong, A. C.
327949 Gnr. Armstrong, H. J.
331928 Cpl. Baillie, J. B.
327910 Dvr. Barnard, G. A.
331870 Sig. Bass, W. H.
331802 Gnr. Barnes, R. D.
331875 Gnr. Barrett, W.
332924 Gnr. Belford, J. J.
327913 Dvr. Birrell, J.
1260350 Dvr. Blogg, J. W.
327957 Dvr. Bowman, H.
332835 Dvr. Bridges, W.
332834 A/Bbdr. Bradley, J.
331894 Cpl.-Sadd. Bridgeman,
        J. N.
331609 Dvr. Browning, F. E.
331889 Gnr. Brunsdale, N. C.
331913 Bbdr. Bryant, C. A.
1260388 Gnr. Burrows, B.
327904 Cpl. Bellingham, A. B.
331914 Sig. Carr, C. B.
327887 Gnr. Carter, A. C.
327970 A/Bbdr. Chambers,
        W. G.
327890 Sig. Champion, D. A.
327882 Gnr. Cheetham,
        J. C. H.
331807 Bbdr. Christianson, T.
331803 Cpl. Clapstone, L.
687185 S/S. Clarke, J. G.
   445 Gnr. Clarke, J. S.
1260352 Dvr. Clayton, G. V. H.
327980 Gnr. Clifford, A.
327934 Gnr. Colchester, W. M.
331805 Gnr. Collier, W. W.
331922 Dvr. Connolly, T.
332896 Gnr. Cook, J.
331806 Dvr. Coupland, A.
331924 Dvr. Crowe, J. P.
331876 Dvr. Currier, F.
327916 Dvr. Davey, W. H.
331808 Gnr. Davies, A.
331890 Sig. Dawson, L. L.
331809 Sgt. Donnan, J. W.

332817 Gnr. de Sausmarez,
        C. A. W.
331882 Cpl. Douglass, L. V.
331810 Gnr. Dow, R.
161233 Dvr. Downie, J.
327874 Gnr. Ellis, E.
327966 Sig. Emerson, R. R.
327958 Cpl. Evans, A. E.
331811 Sig. Faunch, E. J. H.
706149 Dvr. Ferguson, G.
706411 Dvr. Ferguson, R.
327952 Gnr. Field, W. M.
327869 Sig. Finnsson, F.
331813 Dvr. Foreman, J.
534439 Dvr. Fraser, D. S.
331884 A/Bbdr. Fry, J. C.
332861 Dvr. Green, A. R.
Carried for Brigade Hqrs.
332894 Gnr. Gardner, A. N.
331815 Gnr. Gaught, H.
327851 Gnr. Gerrard, W. G.
327885 Whlr. Goswell, E. A.
331816 Cpl.-S/S. Graham, G.
331900 Dvr. Grant, J.
331896 Gnr. Grant, R.
 77952 Dvr. Grassick, J.
1260305 Dvr. Griffin, O. R.
331868 Dvr. Griffiths, S.
331897 A/Bbdr. Hamilton, J.J.
1260368 Gnr. Hamilton, R.
116502 Far.-Sgt. Hardy, M.
327855 Gnr. Hargrave, C.
331898 Dvr. Harrison, T. W.
331879 Dvr. Hayward, V. M.
331921 Gnr. Headrick, W. A.
331770 Dvr. Heatherton, R.
331820 Gnr. Henderson, J. D.
332827 Dvr. Hinchcliffe, W.
331821 Sig. Horspool, G.
327895 Gnr. Howden, C. B.
331919 Dvr. Hudson, T. A.
331822 Bbdr. Hudson, W.
331823 Dvr. Hudson, W. E.
331824 Dvr. Hughes, J. S.
216999 Gnr. Hume, J. M.
331871 Gnr. Ironside, G. L.
331909 Dvr. Johnston, H. O.
1260413 Gnr. Jones, A.
216460 Gnr. Jones, C.
331892 Sdlr. Jones, D. O.
332840 Gnr. Jones, W.
331829 Gnr. Jones, W. H.

7

1260369 Dvr. Kelway, S.	1260391 Dvr. Ross, J. H.
331085 Gnr. Kenwood, F. H.	331866 A/Bbdr. Roy, J. L.
327932 Dvr. Kilgour, J. W.	331886 Dvr. Samson, F. S.
331830 Dvr. King, F. G.	327940 Gnr Sangster, L. A.
327969 Gnr. King, F. R.	327906 Dvr. Scott, C. W.
231040 Gnr. King, G.	331927 Sgt. Scougall, G. H.
331831 A/Cpl. Leys, R.A.	216459 Gnr. Selvage, G. H.
327862 Sgt. Link, N.	116389 Bbdr. Smart, E. H.
331832 Gnr. Lyons, A. H.	231633 Gnr. Smith, A. J.
331839 B.Q.M.S. Manning,T.H	1260412 Dvr. Smith, J. M.
13901 Bbdr. Marshall, S.	331852 Whlr. Smith, P.
331841 Gnr. Martin, B.B.	327918 Dvr. Speers, K. E.
331881 Dvr. Mason, H. R.	331895 Gnr. Sprunt, E. L.
332891 Dvr. Mattin, F.	883686 Dvr. Srigley, R. J.
327857 Dvr. Mayers, F. T.	216844 Gnr. Steen, J.
913018 Dvr. Medlicott, G. G.	331853 Gnr. Stewart, J.
231188 Gnr. Millar, J.	808646 Tptr. Stringer, E. C. O.
331891 Gnr. Miller, D.	331874 Dvr. Stringer, G. J.
331923 Dvr. Mills, I.	736497 Dvr. Sutherland, A.
332892 Dvr. Milne, C. F.	1260439 A/Staff-Sgt.-Fitter
331887 Cpl. Massey, G. A.	Shaw, J. (Carried for
1260416 Dvr. Morry, D. W.	Brigade Hqrs.)
332914 Gnr. McBrady, D. J.	327953 Gnr. Tanner, A. B. W.
331907 Sig. McCauley, H. W.	331854 Dvr. Thomas, W.
327853 Dvr. McCreath, S.	116419 Sig. Thursby, S.
331834 Gnr. MacDonald, J.	331908 Gnr. Turcotte, E. C.
327867 Dvr. McFerran, R. J.	331855 A/Sgt. Turcotte, J. A.
331911 S/S. Mackie, A. J.	116251 Sig. Vallance, D.
331877 Dvr. Mackie, D.	116436 Gnr. Walden, A.
331880 Dvr. McKinnon, M. M.	331915 Dvr. Waldie, J. C.
116182 Sgt. Maclean, J. A.	327893 B.S.M. Walker, E.
331838 Dvr. McLean, R. G.	331883 Sgt. Wallas, W. A.
331837 Bbdr. McNeil, J. E.	331862 Gnr. Wallwork, J. H.
327959 Dvr. McQueen, J.	331905 Dvr. Walshe, R. F.
883647 Gnr. McSpadden,W. H.	231167 Dvr. Watson, R.
331906 Sig. McTeer, D.	331901 Cpl. Weatherley, G.W.
331912 Sig. McTeer, K. G.	331910 Gnr. White, H. A.
327898 Bbdr. Neher, G. G.	327862 Sgt. Williams, W. B.
327881 Dvr. Nicoll, H. L.	332881 Gnr. Wilson, C. S.
331844 Dvr. Owens, G.	327866 A/Bbdr. Wilson, D. W.
331845 Dvr. Page, W.	331860 Dvr. Wolstencroft, J.
331861 Dvr. Paris, R. J. C.	1260430 Bbdr. Wood, J. T.
706561 Dvr. Parkes, F. C.	331863 Bbdr. Woods, J. E.
1260403 Dvr. Pellow, F.	331859 Sgt. Wray, C. F.
327894 A/Bbdr. Patterson, G.	910159 A/Bbdr. Wright, J. M.
327954 S/S. Pennycook, W. A.	327891 A/Bbdr. Young,
332887 Dvr. Piper, P. J.	A. J. W.
331847 A/Bbdr. Powell, A.	
231019 Gnr. Protheroe, E. J. T.	ATTACHED.
327928 A/Bbdr. Pull, J.	524072 Private Ainsley, E. L.
327879 Gnr. Ragotte, G.	(C.A.M.C.)
331849 Gnr. Rennison, G. G.	324919 Vet.-Sgt. Clarke, G. A.
327945 Dvr. Reynolds, L. M.	(C.A.V.C.)
327935 Gnr. Richbell, E.	
1260436 Bbdr. Ritchie, R. A.	CARRIED FOR 5TH DIVISIONAL
332858 Dvr. Roberts, W.	TRAIN DETACHMENT.
180127 Dvr. Rogers, J. E. M.	512835 Dvr. Watts, J. C.
	104620 Dvr. Wilson, J.

DIARY.

21st AUGUST.—Right Half Battery—viz., Major G. S. Browne, Lieuts. Virtue and Babbage, and 101 other ranks—left Milford Station at 5 a.m. with three guns and limbers, six ammunition waggons and limbers, one G.S. waggon, one cook cart, one water cart, and 89 horses. Arrived at Southampton at 7.24 a.m. Left Half Battery—viz., Captain C. H. Collinson, Lieut. A. G. Oliver, and 93 other ranks, left Milford Station at 6.30 a.m. with three guns and limbers, six ammunition waggons and limbers, one G.S. waggon and the balance of the horses, and arrived at Southampton at 7.15 a.m. Lieut. C. H. Locke met the Battery at Southampton. The Battery embarked at South-ampton at 2.30 p.m. and sailed at 4.30 p.m.

22nd AUGUST.—Battery disembarked at Le Havre at 2 p.m. and moved off to No. 1 Rest Camp.

23rd AUGUST.—Entrained at Gare des Marchandices, Havre, during the afternoon. Train left at 8 p.m.

24th AUGUST.—The train was wrecked at Poix. Seven cars off the rails, and one car of horses overturned. Dvr. McQueen, who was in this car, was slightly injured. One firing battery waggon was badly damaged. Train left Poix at 2.50 p.m., and stopped at Abbeville for water. Arrived at Lillers at Midnight.

25th AUGUST.—Detrained and moved off to Ames. Battery bivouacked outside of village. Inspected by Lt.-General Currie during the afternoon.

26th AUGUST.—Rain.

1917.

27th AUGUST.—Major Browne, Lieut. Locke, six Nos. One, four signallers, and one batman leave to be attached to 27th Battery, C.F.A., for instructional purposes in the active operation zone.

28th AUGUST.—Rain.

29th AUGUST.—Inspected by G.O.C., R.A., Canadian Corps. Lieut. G. S. Raley reported for duty, having been detained in England when the Battery left there.

30th AUGUST.—Moved horse lines into the village of Ames. This was necessary owing to the muddy condition of the field. Major Browne and party returned to Battery.

31st AUGUST.—Raining. Cleaning up.

1st SEPTEMBER.—Raining. Pay parade.

2nd SEPTEMBER.—Brigade Church Parade under Capt. Bowen.

3rd SEPTEMBER.—Prepare to move to-morrow.

4th SEPTEMBER.—Battery moved off from Ames at 8.50 a.m. Owing to the Battery moving across a stubble field on a hill about 10.30 a.m. the G.S. waggon (which was heavily loaded) stuck in the soft ground, and was only freed after considerable effort. The Battery arrived at Carency about 9 p.m. and bivouacked. The weather during the day was very fine.

1917.

5th SEPTEMBER.—In the morning Major Browne and Lieuts. Locke, Virtue and Oliver went forward to arrange for the taking over of position from 27th Battery, C.F.A. Later, the Nos. One and Detachments, and C., D., and E. Sub. Guns. went forward, and the three guns were put into action in Cite d'Abbatoir (Lievin). Map Location, M.35 a 70.50.

6th SEPTEMBER.—The Battery was heavily shelled after taking over position last night, gas shells forming part of the material used. Box respirators were worn for two hours. No. 331802 Gnr. R. D. Barnes was seriously wounded to-day and evacuated to England. At the waggon lines the afternoon was spent by the men in erecting shelters of various kinds. About 5.30 p.m. violent rain fell, accompanied by thunder. A., B., and F. Sub. Guns moved up, accompanied by practically the balance of the gunners. The Battery was shelled from 1.30 to 2.30 a.m., again at 8 a.m., and again at 1 a.m. O. Pip duty was taken over by Lieut. Oliver, accompanied by Signallers C. B. Carr and H. W. McCauley. The O. Pip is in the second story of a half ruined house in Cite Riaumont, in front of Lievin and overlooking Lens.

7th SEPTEMBER.—The day developed into a warm, sunny one, and the ground quickly dried. No further casualties. Registering carried on during the day at the Gun Position. "S.O.S." firing on Zone at 10 p.m. This was our first S.O.S. The response was very quick, and the Infantry stated that the effect was most satisfactory.

8th SEPTEMBER.—Our Horse Lines moved from intersection of light railway (along Souchez River) and branch road below Carency Village to lines vacated by the Lahore Battery. These lines are a few hundred yards from Hospital Corner. Map location, X. 22 a 75.85. Very fine weather A heavy Canadian Mail received this evening. Registering carried on during the day, and some harassing fire. Lieut. A. G. Virtue went on Liaison Duty with the Tenth Battalion.

11

1917.

9th SEPTEMBER.—Registering and harassing fire carried out. Church Parade held at the Waggon Lines. Orderly Room established in a "bivvy." used by the O.C. of the Lahore Battery at Waggon Lines. The weather continues fine.

10th SEPTEMBER.—Monday.—Fine weather still continues. Work commenced on building of winter stables. Battery shelled with two or three large shells.

11th SEPTEMBER.—Tuesday.—Weather still continues fine. Nissen hut received and erected at waggon lines, as well as a number of tents. The men moved from dug-outs, shelters, etc., into the tents. Battery to the left very heavily shelled all day. Some splinters dropped on our position. Much aerial activity. Harassing fire on Zone during night.

12th SEPTEMBER.—Wednesday.—Fine, but very windy. Work on stables continued. Sig. D. Vallance very slightly wounded, but able to remain on duty. Heavy shelling in vicinity of Cemetery to rear of Battery Position during day. Harassing fire on Zone during evening, also slow rate of fire S.O.S. on Zone.

13th SEPTEMBER.—Thursday.—Weather continues fine. Work on stables continued. Hostile shelling, mostly 4's (about 50 rounds) 500 yards rear of Battery between 2 and 4 p.m. Three shells on Battery Position from 4.1 gun at 3 p.m. Transferred for tactical purposes to Right Group, under Lieut.-Col. J. S. Stewart.

14th SEPTEMBER.—Friday.—Slight amount of rain to-day. Parade for pay. Enemy aerial activity between the hours of 5 and 7 p.m.

1917.

15th SEPTEMBER.—Saturday.—Sgt. Wallas, Sgt. Donnan, and Sgt. Williams came down from the gun position for the first time. Work on the stables continued. Hostile 'planes appeared at intervals during the day. Heavy shelling at 7 p.m. in 29 d. Apparently 4.1 and some 5.9.

16th SEPTEMBER.—Sunday.—At the waggon lines the Battery paraded to attend Funeral Service for Gunner McClellan, 60th Battery—the first man to be killed in the Brigade. Bathing parade in the afternoon. The Battery Position was heavily shelled between the hours of 12.45 p.m. and 8 p.m. About 125 rounds, mostly 5.9's H.E. No. 3 pit damaged, but no damage to gun. Our Nissen Hut at the waggon lines was removed by the Engineers.

17th SEPTEMBER.—Monday.—Three 8-inch shells dropped in rear of the Battery Position during the morning.

18th SEPTEMBER.—Tuesday.—Weather continues fine. Work continued on the Stables. The 60th Battery are building stables near ours, but higher up the hill, and have been working at them for some days. Some shelling on our right flank. Also at Cemetery at left rear of Battery.

19th SEPTEMBER.—Wednesday.—Weather continues fine and warm, but a little windy. Bathing parade for men who had no bath on Sunday, at waggon lines. The three sergeants referred to on 15th inst. returned to the guns, together with about 20 men to release others for rest purposes.

20th SEPTEMBER.—Thursday.—Weather still continues fine. Work on stables continued.

21st SEPTEMBER.—Friday.—Quiet at the Battery Position. Owing to a gas attack on our left flank and in rear we had some gas over our position and wore our box respirators for a time. The gas was brought across by the wind.

1917.

22nd SEPTEMBER.—Saturday.—Magnificent weather still continues. Quiet at Battery Position.

23rd SEPTEMBER.—Sunday.—Considerable aerial activity. Capt. Collinson arrived at Battery Position. Sgt. J. A. Turcotte left for waggon lines for the first time, and Gnr. Rennison took over work of O.R. Clerk at guns. Work on stables continued.

24th SEPTEMBER.—Monday.—Weather still continues good. Quiet, but considerable aerial activity. Good progress being made on tunnelling at Battery Position.

25th SEPTEMBER.—Tuesday.—All quiet last night. Six enemy balloons up this morning, and hauled down in the afternoon. Enemy 'planes overhead during the afternoon, directing fire on a Battery to our left. Battery to our rear shelled with 5.9's in the afternoon, but not heavily. Work continued on stables.

26th SEPTEMBER.—Wednesday.—Weather still keeps fine. Quiet at Battery Position. Work at the stables continued.

27th SEPTEMBER.—Thursday.—No shooting, except calibration, carried out to-day, and there was no hostile shelling of our immediate area. Positions on our left were shelled during the day, 5.9's being used about 8.15 p.m. About 5.10 p.m. an enemy aeroplane flew over our position and set fire to one of our observation balloons. The enemy airman returned to his own lines pursued by several British machines. At 6.50 p.m. another enemy aeroplane flew across and set on fire a second balloon. He was attacked by several British machines and forced to descend (after sharp fighting) in our lines. The Hun airman was a poor sport. When the balloon caught fire the two observers jumped and came down by parachute, and this exponent of Kultur fired at them while they were helpless in mid-air. However, he missed them.

14

1917.

28th SEPTEMBER.—Friday.—Considerable aerial activity, but nothing else of much importance. The signallers' dug-out was completed. Weather continues fine.

29th SEPTEMBER.—Saturday.—A very quiet and uneventful day in every respect. The day was dull and hazy during the greater portion of the time, and aerial activity was almost nil. Only one enemy balloon up—about 6 p.m.

30th SEPTEMBER.—Sunday.—Another very quiet day. Weather continues fine. Work at waggon lines continued.

1st OCTOBER.—Monday.—Still very quiet at Battery Position. Sgt. Turcotte arrived back there in the evening.

2nd OCTOBER.—Tuesday.—Sgt. Turcotte relieved Gnr. Rennison, who returned to the waggon lines. Quiet day. Fine weather continues. Slight shelling rear of Battery Position. Harassing fire carried out night of 2nd-3rd October.

3rd OCTOBER.—Wednesday.—Weather cloudy. Capt. Collinson left for gun position. The Hun shelled us again to-day, using 5.9's. A piece from an air burst hit Dvr. W. Roberts in the hand, and he was evacuated to hospital.

4th OCTOBER.—Thursday.—Horses moved into new stables. The Major returned from the guns to waggon lines. The Battery received orders to change position, and the right section was relieved by the right section of the 5th Battery late at night (Major Alderson). Heavy rain during the afternoon. Weather fair at Battery Position. Some shelling near Battery Position. Fire on S.O.S. line, also on target "Retaliation Left" during evening.

15

1917.

5th OCTOBER.—Friday.—Weather good. Much shelling at Battery Position at Cite d'Abbatoir, mostly 5.9's. Remaining sections, guns, and all personnel retired to waggon lines. Position handed over to O.C. 5th Battery, C.F.A. Fighting maps, intelligence, aeroplane photos, etc., handed over to him. Right section guns and personnel and portion of Headquarters party move up to a position in Cite de la Plaine (Map location, M.15 d 90.70) occupied by "A" Battery, 112th Brigade, R.F.A. This position is in an open field, in trenches.

6th OCTOBER.—Saturday.—A wet day. Moved remaining four guns into new position and took over position from A/112 R.F.A. The Battery passed under the tactical control of the 24th Brigade, R.F.A. on this date. We now have our O. Pip in Fosse II. Fired 50 rounds harassing fire during night.

7th OCTOBER.—Sunday.—Weather cold, with continuous rain. No hostile shelling. Fired 36 rounds at target given by Brigade at 10 a.m. Fired 50 rounds harassing fire during night 7th-8th October.

8th OCTOBER.—Monday.—Weather poor; showers during the day. No hostile shelling. Fired the usual 50 rounds harassing fire to-night.

9th OCTOBER.—Tuesday.—Weather cold, and raining a little. Stock for the Battery canteen purchased.

10th OCTOBER.—Wednesday.—Battery moved to new position in Cite de Rollencourt ("White Chateau"). (Map location, M.27 b 90.65.) Much shelling on our right flank. Handed over all ammunition on hand at position to 60th Battery C.F.A. The Battery canteen opened to-day.

1917.

11th OCTOBER.—Thursday.—Nothing of importance to record. Weather somewhat colder.

12th OCTOBER.—Friday.—Wettish day. Nothing of great importance to record.

13th OCTOBER.—Saturday.—A wet day. The Right Section, guns, and personnel, moved to new position at M.23 a 00.27, in Lievin, 300 yards east of Fosse 3 de Lievin.

14th OCTOBER.—Sunday.—Centre and Left Sections moved to new position in Constitution Hill (Lievin) at M.7 c 45.40. Weather fine. No church parade.

15th OCTOBER.—Monday.—Fine day. Nothing of importance to record.

16th OCTOBER.—Tuesday.—Fine day, but windy. Waggon lines moved to Sains en Gohelle.

17th OCTOBER.—Wednesday.—Weather continues very windy, but fine. Moving to new waggon lines continued.

18th OCTOBER.—Thursday.—Weather fine. Moving to new lines continued.

1917.

19th OCTOBER.—Friday.—A general " strafe," beginning at about 5 p.m. Fired on S.O.S. line for about an hour and fifty minutes. Considerable hostile shelling during this period, mostly " whizz-bangs." Finished moving the waggon lines.

20th OCTOBER.—Saturday.—Weather fine. Nothing of special interest to record.

21st OCTOBER.—Sunday.—**883647** Gnr. W. H. McSpadden very seriously wounded while out collecting wire, and evacuated to a dressing station, where he died.

22nd OCTOBER.—Monday.—**331896** Gnr. R. Grant accidentally killed while dismantling a house at the Right Section Gun position. This work was being done to increase field of fire.

23rd OCTOBER.—Tuesday.—Double funeral for the two gunners killed on 21st and 22nd. Map spotting of graves is Sheet 36B. Location R.2 d 40.40. This cemetery lies between our Gun Park and the village of Fosse 10 on the right-hand side of the road, going to Fosse 10.

24th OCTOBER.—Wednesday.—Weather windy. Nothing particular to record.

25th OCTOBER.—Thursday.—The Major went down to the waggon lines. The weather is cold but fine.

1917.

26th OCTOBER.—Friday.—Rainy. Nothing special.

27th OCTOBER.—Saturday.—Fine day. Lieut. Locke went down to waggon lines.

28th OCTOBER.—Sunday.—Weather continues to be fine. Church Parade.

29th OCTOBER.—Monday.—Weather fine. Nothing special.

30th OCTOBER.—Tuesday. Rather rainy. Nothing special.

31st OCTOBER.—Wednesday.—Fine day and quite warm. Heavy shelling of our position at Constitution Hill, which started at 8 a.m. and lasted till about 6 p.m. The communication trench between the guns and the officers' mess was badly damaged, and the landscape generally had an entirely different appearance to what it had before the show started. No one hurt.

1st NOVEMBER.—Thursday.—Weather still continues fine. The men at the waggon lines attended a Ceremonial Parade in memory of British and French soldiers killed in the War.

2nd NOVEMBER.—Friday.—Another fine day. Nothing of special interest.

1917.

3rd NOVEMBER.—Saturday.—Weather still continues to be fine.

4th NOVEMBER.—Sunday.—Parade for pay at the waggon lines. Otherwise nothing unusual.

5th NOVEMBER.—Monday.—Nothing of special importance.

6th NOVEMBER.—Tuesday.—Weather still mild. Otherwise nothing special.

7th NOVEMBER.—Wednesday.—Nothing of special interest.

8th NOVEMBER.—Thursday.—Nothing of special interest.

9th NOVEMBER.—Friday.—Nothing of special interest.

10th NOVEMBER.—Saturday.—A very cold day. Raid carried out on trenches of enemy by infantry. About 960 rounds expended by this Battery. Battery passes from control of 78th Field Artillery Brigade to 13th Brigade, C.F.A. Right Section and personnel moved to new position G34C 80.10. Near Maroc.

11th NOVEMBER.—Sunday.—Control of Battery passes from 13th Brigade, C.F.A. to Loos Group (Lieut.-Col. A. T. Ogilvie) at 12 noon. Centre and Left Sections move to new position G34C 80.10, near Maroc. Very quiet. Our O.P. is now in Hurdle Trench on top of Hill 70.

1917.

12th NOVEMBER.—Monday.—Weather still fine. Registration carried out on Zero point.

13th-16th NOVEMBER.—Nothing of importance, except that the weather remains very fine.

17th NOVEMBER.—Saturday.—Firing carried out on crash targets. Carried from 5.30 to 7.15 as ordered by Group.

18th NOVEMBER.—Sunday.—Registration on Zero carried out. Pay day at waggon lines.

19th NOVEMBER.—Monday.—Opportunity targets fired on by Battery.

20th NOVEMBER.—Tuesday.—A little registering and some sniping on movement carried out. Weather continues fine.

21st NOVEMBER.—Wednesday.—Nothing of importance. Our O.P. is now " Craigowen," on high ground north of Hill 70, a wonderful place for sniping.

22nd NOVEMBER.—Thursday.—Fired on S.O.S. lines at 6.15 a.m. Some 366 rounds of shrapnel expended.

23rd NOVEMBER.—Friday.—Very quiet all day. Sniping on two targets. Much aerial activity during the afternoon.

1917.

24th NOVEMBER.—Saturday.—Very quiet. Some sniping on movement. Weather good.

25th NOVEMBER.—Sunday.—Weather bad. Snow in afternoon.
Situation very quiet.

26th NOVEMBER.—Monday.—Fine day. Right Section and personnel came out of action and returned to waggon lines at
Sains-en-Gohelle.

27th NOVEMBER.—Tuesday.—Rainy. Balance of Battery came
out of action and returned to waggon lines.

28th NOVEMBER.—Wednesday.—Complete Battery at waggon
lines. Weather fine. Major G. S. Browne (O.C.) went to
hospital with trench fever.

29th NOVEMBER.—Thursday.—Weather very fine and mild.
Battery still out of action.

30th NOVEMBER.—Friday.—Still mild. Right Section and personnel moved to new position near Annequin, G11 b 45.54.
This is on the La Bassee front.

1st DECEMBER.—Saturday.—Battery moved to new waggon lines
at Verquigneul, just off the Arras-Bethune Road. Centre
and Left Sections went into action. The weather changed,
turning very cold.

2nd DECEMBER.—Sunday.—Weather very cold and windy.

1917.

3rd DECEMBER.—Monday.—Weather still very cold and frosty. Left Section moved to A20 a 30.67 owing to the very poor condition of their gunpits and the fact that there was no cover for personnel. This position is in an orchard. The family still occupy the house and refuse to leave in spite of the danger of our guns attracting hostile fire.

4th DECEMBER.—Tuesday.—This vicinity bombed by enemy aeroplanes about 9 p.m.

5th DECEMBER.—Wednesday.—Another bombing raid by enemy aeroplane. This time about 4.45 p.m. Canteen re-opened. Our O.P. is in second story of a brick house in eastern outskirts of Cambrin. A very cold place.

6th DECEMBER.—Thursday.—Still cold, but fine.

7th DECEMBER.—Friday.—Decided change in the weather. Quite warm to-day. Bethune subjected to shelling.

8th DECEMBER.—Saturday.—Weather continues mild. Nothing of special interest to note.

9th DECEMBER.—Sunday.—Weather rainy.

10th DECEMBER.—Monday.—Weather fine. Capt. Collinson and A/Sgt. J. A. Turcotte opened the Poll at the waggon lines, and a considerable number of the Battery voted.

1917.

11th DECEMBER.—Tuesday.—Polling of votes in the Dominion Election continued. Weather fine.

12th DECEMBER.—Wednesday.—Material drawn from Bethune to erect wind screens for the horse standings. Another raid by enemy aeroplanes.

13th DECEMBER.—Thursday.—Work on erection of wind screens commenced.

14th DECEMBER.—Friday.—Rainy again. Arrangements now in force whereby the men eat in several estaminets.

15th DECEMBER.—Saturday.—Weather fine again. Enemy aeroplanes again dropped bombs in the vicinity.

16th DECEMBER.—Sunday.—Weather still mild. Nothing of importance to record.

17th DECEMBER.—Monday.—Weather very cold again, with a heavy fall of snow during the night.

18th DECEMBER.—Tuesday.—Weather very cold. Enemy aeroplanes again bombed in this vicinity.

19th DECEMBER.—Wednesday. Weather still very cold.

1917.

21st DECEMBER.—Friday.—Arrangements being made to shift waggon lines. Q.M.S. Manning and Gnr. Faunch leave for England on Special Christmas Leave.

22nd DECEMBER.—Saturday.—Weather still very cold. Advance party left for former waggon lines in Sains-en-Gohelle. Canteen closed and moved over. S.S. Mackie leaves on Christmas Leave.

23rd DECEMBER.—Sunday.—Balance of Battery moved over from Verquigneul. Cold. Guns handed over to Imperial Battery taken over. Fired rounds to date 13,703. We lost our original guns brought from England at this transfer owing to the new system introduced to facilitate the exchange of positions.

24th DECEMBER.—Monday.—Advance party left for new position at M29 a 62.55, Cite de Bureaux. Christmas dinner held at the waggon lines, for which turkeys were purchased from the funds. The Battery went into action at night, the main position being at Cite de Bureaux, and the Centre Section (which was detached) being at M30 c 12.11, in the side of the railway enbankment about three hundred yards ahead of our old Cite d'Abbatoir position. (Cite de Bureaux is in the vicinity of Bois-de-Riaumont.)

25th DECEMBER.—Tuesday.—Mild early in the day, followed by a heavy fall of snow.

26th DECEMBER.—Wednesday.—Weather very cold. Our waggon lines were stripped of everything moveable when we left for Verquigneul, and are in poor shape.

27th DECEMBER.—Thursday.—Still very cold. Arrangements being made to obtain material for repair of lines, etc.

1917.

28th DECEMBER.—Friday.—Frost still very severe.

29th DECEMBER.—Saturday.—Weather still severe. Several cases of scabies lately in the Battery.

30th DECEMBER.—Sunday.—Weather cold.

31st DECEMBER.—Monday.—Weather still cold.

1918.

1st JANUARY.—Tuesday.—Weather cold. No shelling.

2nd JANUARY.—Wednesday.—Still very cold. Good observation, and many enemy balloons in sight.

3rd JANUARY.—Thursday.—Weather still cold. Slag being hauled to improve paths, etc., in lines. Considerable activity on our front. Many enemy balloons up.

4th JANUARY.—Friday.—Still cold. Nothing very important at lines. Quiet. Observation fair. Guns were calibrated to-day.

5th JANUARY.—Saturday.—Frost thawing. Work being done to use half of cinema billet as a messroom. Dull day. Poor observation, and very quiet.

6th JANUARY.—Sunday.—Weather has turned very cold again. Snowed in afternoon. Quiet.

1918.

7th JANUARY.—Monday.—Weather rainy and damp. Q.M.S. Manning and Gnr. Faunch reported back from leave.

8th JANUARY.—Tuesday.—Weather cold and frosty again. Work proceeding on erection of protection of horse standings against bomb raids.

9th JANUARY.—Wednesday.—Nothing of special importance at lines. Weather cold and clear.

10th JANUARY.—Thursday.—A thaw accompanied by a high wind.

11th JANUARY.—Friday.—Weather cold. Major Greene took over as acting O.C. during Major Browne's absence.

12th JANUARY.—Saturday.—Thawing again to-day. Work on protection barricades proceeding. Slag being hauled these days.

13th JANUARY.—Sunday.—Weather cold again.

14th JANUARY.—Monday.—More snow to-day. Special gas drill for a few days to speed up for test.

15th JANUARY.—Tuesday.—Very wet and stormy. Some shelling by enemy of positions in rear of waggon lines.

16th JANUARY.—Wednesday.—Again wet, accompanied by very high wind. More enemy shelling in rear of lines.

1918.

17th JANUARY.—Thursday.—Another wet day. Enemy again shelling positions in rear of lines.

18th JANUARY.—Friday.—Battery Position shelled with 4.1's from 12.30 p.m. on. Gnr. C. S. Wilson wounded and admitted to dressing station. Lieut. Babbage, who is on 14 days' leave, got an extension of nine days.

19th JANUARY.—Saturday.—Fair day. Not doing quite so much harassing fire these days. The Hun shelled us intermittently all day and during the night. No damage done.

20th JANUARY.—Sunday.—Yesterday we took over six guns and a few stores from the 18th Battery. To-night two of these guns were put into a new four-gun position at M22 b 90.78 (Constitution Hill, Lievin), which we are building.

21st JANUARY.—Monday.—Weather a bit drizzly. The 12th Battery, C.F.A., under Capt. Steele, took over our Right Section this evening and our men went over to the new position. Four more guns came up to-night, two to the main position and two behind Fosse 3 at M.22 B 58.18.

22nd JANUARY.—Tuesday.—We were relieved completely at 12 noon to-day, handing over indents to cover all deficiencies and obtaining receipts. A fair day. We moved over to the new position, of which four of the pits are built right into the side of one block of some of the miners' houses. The Left Section are at the Fosse. Men relieved to-day. Our team got into trouble at the Fosse to-night, owing to shelling by 4.2 howitzer, one horse being killed, one so wounded that it died, another badly wounded, and the fourth horse just touched. He could just walk home. The V.O. came up, but left it to us to shoot the nag. Corp. Weatherley and the drivers did good work in getting the team clear.

1918.

23rd JANUARY.—Wednesday.—A fair day. The General was up·
this a.m. We got up 600 rounds A.X. and sent over to the·
Fosse 150 rounds, 48 A. and 102 A.X. from a dump we
found here. Our S.O.S. Zone is covering Cinnibar Trench
from M.14 A.80.78 to N.8 D.62.75. We registered numbers·
1, 2, and 3 guns to-day on the water tower, also 2 on S.1, a
sniping target just north-east of water-tower. The H.F. was.
cancelled in evening. We got up 1,200 rounds (600 A. and
600 A.X.) to-night.

24th JANUARY.—Thursday.—Had an S.O.S. slow rate early this.
a.m. Working on the pits. We have quite a lot of mate-·
rial, but we use it all. Hope to be 5.9-proof soon.

25th JANUARY.—Friday.—Lieut. Raley went up to 1st Inf. Bde..
at Cite Ste. Pierre as L.O. for seven days. Lieut. Quinn
O'Pipping from Fosse 3. Fair visibility.

26th JANUARY.—Saturday.—Foggy and quiet day. Work progres-·
sing on pits. Lieut. Quinn as L.O. at 1st Battalion.

27th JANUARY.—Sunday.—Foggy, quiet day. Lieut. Stanton at O.P·
on Riaumont. Visibility no good. O.C. visited first Battalion
re prospective raid. Nothing definitely settled.

28th JANUARY.—Monday.—Work on pits held up for lack of de-
livery of iron rails. 500 rounds A. received last night and
400 A. and 200 A.X. to-night. Our complement is 450 per
gun—in all 2,700, 75 per cent. A. and 25 per cent. A.X. Fair
visibility. Lieut. Virtue at O.P. O.C. went through Cite
Jean d'Arc looking for O.P. Collected salvaged pit props,
etc., in the evening. Rails came up last night. Quiet night.

29th JANUARY.—Tuesday.—Fair visibility. O.C. reconnoitred for
new O.P. up Crocodile Trench, but without much success.
Fairly quiet day. Work on gun pits progressing. Lieut.
Quinn returned yesterday from 1st Batt. L.O.

1918.

30th JANUARY.—Wednesday.—Poor visibility. O.C. and Lieut. Virtue shot from Crocodile Trench near railway cutting, on Zero, but very difficult to see. Quiet day. The enemy is exceptionally quiet, especially with his artillery in the direction of Lievin. Rails came up to-night.

31st JANUARY.—Thursday.—Very misty all day. Cold and damp. Wind from the east. Quiet on the Front. Moon is waning. Lieut. Sherlock, D.G.O., is staying here for a week. Work progressing on pits. Working Party returned to Waggon Lines to-night. Lieut. Raley returned from Brigade L.O.

1st FEBRUARY.—Friday.—General Thacker, C.R.A., 1st C.D.A., honoured us with an inspection at guns this a.m. Things seemed satisfactory. Dull day.

2nd FEBRUARY.—Saturday.—Dull day. General Morrison, G.O.C., R.A., Can. Corps, inspected Waggon Lines, and seemed pleased with the lay-out.

3rd FEBRUARY.—Sunday.—Fair day. Lieut. Stanton at 4th Battalion H.Q. as L.O. Checked the S.O.S. Lines.

4th FEBRUARY.—Monday.—Good visibility towards noon. Were able to calibrate all our guns on the water-tower with excellent results. No. 1 is 1580; No. 2 is 1570; No. 3 is 1560; No. 4 is 1580; No. 5 is 1630; No. 6 is 1620 f.s. M.V. Work on the gun position progressing. Speaking-tubes are now in. Lieut. Babbage returned from 24 days' leave on the 1st, and Lieut. Locke returned on the 31st January from 14 days' leave.

5th FEBRUARY.—Tuesday.—Fair visibility. Checked registration on Cinnibar Trench in anticipation of our raid to-morrow evening. Our O.P. is now in second storey of a half-ruined house in Cite Riaumont. There is a ladder for quick descent, and the signallers have instructions to keep a sharp look-out for a slippery pole.

1918.

6th to 22nd FEBRUARY.—Very quiet. . Weather cold, but good on the whole. We are working every day making the pits stronger. Working on Red Line position.

23rd FEBRUARY.—Saturday.—The front has been fairly quiet until now. Fair weather.

24th FEBRUARY.—Sunday.—Fair visibility. Allowed only 50 rounds per day.

25th FEBRUARY.—Monday.—Observation fair. Weather fine; a few showers. Fireplace completed in Office. Inspection at Waggon Lines by A.D.V.S.

26th FEBRUARY.—Tuesday.—Observation good. Visited Cite Calonne position M.13. D.4.0—2—0. Sgt. Evans expects to be finished in two days. Enemy artillery active this evening. Q.M.S. reported at Battery position to check up the work of his assistant. Major Greene on leave to England. Col. Ogilvie says we are to go out for rest on 10/3/18. Must first complete work now under way and repair pits at alternative position at M.17 C.41.37.

27th FEBRUARY.—Wednesday.—Captain Collinson went to Bobs O.P. with Padre Latimer, who came up for a visit and to see the sights. Considerable shelling on both sides of Lens—Lievin Road. A large splinter lit on the roadway near Captain Collinson and the Padre, making a heavy thud. The Padre said, "Captain Collinson, did you hear *that dud* ?" Observation good. Plenty of artillery activity. 200 rounds hauled to L.X. Gnr. Rennison moved over to-day.

1918.

28th FEBRUARY.—Thursday.—Observation not good. Inspected alternative position at M.17 C.42-50 and found things in none too good a shape.

1st MARCH.—Friday.—Observation fair. Weather cool. Strong winds. O.C. inspected Cite Calonne position and found work nearly completed. Went to Waggon Lines.

2nd MARCH.—Saturday.—Cold and foggy. Afternoon stormy; some snow. A splendid inspection at Waggon Lines. Working parties at Cite Calonne sent back to Waggon Lines.

3rd MARCH.—Sunday.—Misty and stormy. Farrier-Sgt. Hardy reported with a small working party to repair damage done to alternative battery position. 49 rounds per day for sniping, exclusive of harassing fire. Bdr. White sets up signs at rear positions.

4th MARCH.—Monday.—Very cloudy. 6.03 a.m. S.O.S., continued until 7.16 a.m. Major Kent killed. Some gas came over. Enemy raid on our right. 21st Batt. in Line. Over 900 rounds fired during S.O.S. Mr. Virtue goes to Waggon Lines; Q.M.S. goes to Waggon Lines. 600 A. and 600 A.X. coming up to-night.

5th MARCH.—Tuesday.—Visibility poor until noon. Fair afternoon.

6th MARCH.—Wednesday.—Visibility poor.

7th MARCH.—Thursday.—Visibility poor. Platforms and trail baulks completed at "C.C.L. XV." First men left on leave to Paris.

1918.

8th MARCH.—Friday.—Visibility good. Inspected by General Mercier, G.O.C., R.A. 1st Army, accompanied by General Morrison and General Dodds.

9th MARCH.—Saturday.—Visibility good. New gas put over on our front. 70 men affected and sent back on morning of 10th.

10th MARCH.—Sunday.—Visibility poor until about 2 p.m. Calibrated No. 2 gun. Captain Daws inspected his new home. Moved Left Section to position near Whizz-bang Corner.

11th MARCH.—Monday.—Visibility good about noon. Registered Left Section for line.

12th MARCH.—Tuesday.—Visibility good after 11 a.m. Mr. Babbage reported from Riding Course. Brigadier-Generals Panet and Dodds, with Colonel Ogilvie, paid a visit of inspection to the Battery.

13th MARCH.—Wednesday.—Visibility good after 12 noon. Lieut. Nesbitt, from relieving battery, reported. Working party started to dig pits in Reserve Position near Bully-Grenay.

14th MARCH.—Thursday.—Captain Daws arrived. Main Position relieved. Lieut. Raley, with 45 other ranks from Division, went to Boulogne Remount Depot for 89 horses on the 12th. Major Greene reported back from 14 days' leave. We were relieved by the 18th Battery C.F.A.

15th MARCH.—Friday.—Battery proceeded to its rest billet at Fosse 6, Bruay Area, for a month's refit and reorganisation. Weather has been wonderfully fine. Remainder of the men of Left Section followed, getting to billets after midnight.

1918.

16th MARCH.—Saturday.—Fine weather and bright sunshine. Spent a.m. cleaning up and locating billets. Three men proceeded to Lievin as working party for wood for new cookhouse. Obtained two G.S. waggons of coal from Calonne.

17th MARCH.—Sunday.—Church service at Haillicourt. Baseball game with 3rd C.D.M.T., which we lost 11 to 4.

18th MARCH.—Monday.—Fine day; south wind. Dipped all our horses at Barlin in the a.m. for microbes. Gun-laying and fixing lines.

19th MARCH.—Tuesday.—Wet day. Exercise ride and work round stables. Got word in the evening that we are to go out to Aire as an Illustration Battery, or some such thing, at the Army School there.

20th MARCH.—Wednesday.—Wet in a.m. Cleared up a bit later. Early a.m. on ride. Captain Collinson left on leave. Men passed their gas in p.m. at Haillicourt. Pay Parade in evening.

21st MARCH.—Thursday.—Misty in a.m. Cleared up later on. Preparations made to move to Aire. This move was cancelled in evening, and orders received to move to Servins instead and to be ready to move at 12 noon to-morrow. This is on account of the great German offensive.

22nd MARCH.—Friday.—Fine day, but misty. Battery moved at noon to Guay Servins and halted for the night.

1918.

23rd MARCH.—Thursday.—Fine day. Moved back into our old Horse Lines in Sains-en-Gohelle, the Battery moving into action in a trench position slightly in front of Maroc. Took over from 7th Battery, C.F.A. This is the position near Maroc previously occupied by us.

24th MARCH.—Sunday.—Nothing very special.

25th MARCH.—Monday.—Work commenced on completion of tunnel under the road, left unfinished by 7th Battery.

26th MARCH.—Tuesday.—Quiet to-day.

27th MARCH.—Wednesday.—Quiet again to-day. The Left Section was relieved by the Honourable Artillery Company and returned to Waggon Lines.

28th MARCH.—Thursday.—Relieved by Honourable Artillery Company *in situ.* Personnel returned to Waggon Lines. Raining a good deal in the evening. Orders to move to-morrow.

29th MARCH.—Friday.—Move cancelled, or rather postponed, and the opportunity was taken to have a bathing parade. Weather fine.

30th MARCH.—Saturday.—A cold day, afterwards turning to heavy rain. Battery moved from Sains-en-Gohelle to Waggon Lines in open field near Maroeuil, the guns moving up into action in Ouse Alley (just off the plank road) at A.18 d. Guns covered with camouflage. We are in front of Roclincourt, just south of Thélus.

1918.

31st MARCH.—Sunday.—Bright, sunny day. Considerable amount of work done digging shallow pits for the guns. "A" Sub. gun moved forward to position alongside Tired Alley. Moved our Waggon Lines from the open field (in which we camped yesterday) to the Veterinary Hospital ("The Dip") on the Arras—Bethune Road, west of Ecurie, where there is a cover for men and horses.

1st APRIL.—Monday.—Another fine day. Gun positions improved. A German airman shot down four of our observation balloons in a row. Battery drew material from the R.E. Dump at Roclincourt.

2nd APRIL.—Tuesday.—Weather continues fine. A good deal of ammunition being hauled at present, the D.A.C. assisting. Lieut. C. G. Quinn reported to the 58th Battery, C.F.A.

3rd APRIL.—Wednesday.—Weather cooler and rainy. More material hauled from R.E. Dump to guns.

4th APRIL.—Thursday.—Weather again uncertain. Work continued on improvement of position. Ammunition still being hauled.

5th APRIL.—Friday.—Fired on counter-preparation soon after 5 a.m. this morning. In retaliatory fire which followed, several shells landed near Battery Position, and one killed No. 1260430 Bdr. J. T. Wood, and wounded H. L. Nicoll (seriously), A. Clifford and E. Richbell (slightly). A small fragment penetrated Cpl. Woods' pocket-book, but did not injure him. Weather rainy.

6th APRIL.—Saturday.—Bdr. J. T. Wood buried to-day at Mont-St.-Eloi cemetery.

1918.

7th APRIL.—Sunday.—Rainy. It was decided to build a new position in rear of our present one, some 500 yards back. Work begun at once.

8th APRIL.—Monday.—Work pushed ahead on new position. New position can be made fairly strong, is well concealed, and there is a large tunnel for personnel. "B" and "C" guns moved. Our forward gun fired 300 rounds of H.F. to-night.

9th APRIL.—Tuesday.—Yesterday and to-day rather misty and foggy—particularly to-day. Work going ahead on new position called "The Castle." We fired at 4.30 a.m. for two hours in support of a raid. Moved our Waggon Lines to alongside Maroeuil cemetery.

10th APRIL.—Wednesday.—"D" and "F" guns moved to the "Castle Position," and personnel moved over. Control and Orderly Room moved. "E" Sub. gun remains as sniper. Moved Waggon Lines to alongside Arras-Bethune Road, north of La Targette.

11th APRIL.—Thursday.—Fine day. Guns registered to-day. Received orders to move to-morrow.

12th APRIL.—Friday.—Handed over to 11th Battery, C.F.A., and took over from 39th Battery, C.F.A., *in situ*, near La Folie Farm, on top of Vimy Ridge. Two guns at S.28 b 70.90, two at T.19 a 80.70, and two at T.19 b 50.40. Water-cart lost for some time.

13th APRIL.—Saturday.—Nothing very special. Usual period of sitting down. Owing to very scattered position it was decided to have a re-arrangement of the guns—one gun to be left forward for sniping and the others brought back. Moved our Waggon Lines to a field near Berthonval Farm.

1918.

14th APRIL.—Sunday.—One gun handed over to 66th Battery and one gun received from them at Main Position.

15th APRIL.—Monday.—Nothing very special. Very cold. No firing.

16th APRIL.—Tuesday.—Nothing very important.

17th APRIL.—Wednesday.—Weather fine to-day. This position is very quiet. The guns are placed at such a range that the front can only be reached when the wind is from our rear. The Forward Section is in front of Vimy Village, and well within normal range. We are O-Pipping from top of Vimy Ridge.

18th APRIL.—Thursday.—Very wet and miserable to-day. Captain Collinson came up, and Major Greene went to the Waggon Lines for a change.

19th APRIL.—Friday.—Snowstorm this morning, and very cold.

20th APRIL.—Saturday.—Owing to our range in Main Position, Calibration from this point is impossible. To-night one gun will be taken forward to T.19 a 10-95, calibrated to-morrow, returned to-morrow night, and another gun taken forward.

21st APRIL.—Sunday.—Weather cold. Another gun taken forward for calibration.

1918.

22nd APRIL.—Monday.—Weather finer. Calibration of guns continued.

23rd APRIL.—Tuesday.—Weather fairly fine. Nothing very special.

24th APRIL.—Wednesday.—Weather only fair. The O.C. returned to the guns and Captain Collinson to the Waggon Lines.

25th APRIL.—Thursday.—Weather fine. Thunder and heavy rain last night. Lieut. C. E. M. Richer reported for duty and went forward to Battery Position.

26th APRIL.—Friday.—Weather very foggy. It has been decided to build new position at rear of present one about 200 yards back, with a view of obtaining pits of good construction and with some concealment.

27th APRIL.—Saturday.—Misty in morning, but improved later. Work on new position proceeding.

28th APRIL.—Sunday.—Very foggy and misty. Nothing of importance.

29th APRIL.—Monday.—Also foggy to-day. Nothing special.

30th APRIL.—Tuesday —Very rainy to-day.

1918.

1st MAY.—Wednesday.—Fine to-day. There is very little to report at this position.

2nd MAY.—Thursday.—Weather beautiful to-day. Captain Holmes à Court, who has been attached to us for several days from the Infantry, left.

3rd MAY.—Friday.—Fine again to-day. Nothing special. Usual harassing fire carried out these nights.

4th MAY.—Saturday.—Weather fine. Right Section relieved by 504th Battery, R.F.A., *in situ*. Forward gun and "B" Sub. personnel relieved returned to Waggon Lines.

5th MAY.—Sunday.—Balance of Battery relieved by 504th R.F.A., and all personnel returned to Waggon Lines. Battery vacated Waggon Lines at 11 p.m. with order to march to Divion, near Houdain.

6th MAY.—Monday.—After marching all night, Battery arrived at Divion about 6.30 a.m. Horse Lines on hill above Divion. Horses and men very tired.

7th MAY.—Tuesday.—Heavy rain in a.m., but fine later. The day spent cleaning up.

8th MAY.—Wednesday.—Beautiful day. The training while here pays considerable attention to R.O. Scouts and to methods of open warfare.

1918.

9th MAY.—Thursday.—B.C. Party went out to Bois de Dames. Remainder cleaning up and gun-laying.

10th MAY.—Friday.—Nothing extraordinary. Just the same sort of work. The weather is fine.

11th MAY.—Saturday.—Fairly fine day. Battery out in the field on Mounted Parade.

12th MAY.—Sunday.—Fine day. Battery out on Mounted Parade all day.

13th MAY.—Monday.—Raining. Canadian mail in. Day spent cleaning up. Pay Parade.

14th MAY.—Tuesday.—Very fine day. Weather has turned very warm. Our guns were taken to Petewawa Range and calibrated by the screen system.

15th MAY.—Wednesday.—Mounted Parade for the Battery. Training along open warfare lines.

16th MAY.—Thursday.—Bathing Parade for the men. General cleaning up of harness and waggons.

17th MAY.—Friday.—Battery out on Mounted Parade. Word received of inspection by G.O.C. Canadian Corps to-morrow. Battery came in early. Very hot day, with brilliant sunshine.

1918.

18th MAY.—Saturday.—Reveille at 4 a.m., and Battery moved off to inspection ground at 8 a.m. Very hot day; hazy. Inspected by General Sir Arthur Currie. Colonel Newlands (formerly our Brigade Major) was with the inspecting party. 52nd Battery, 13th Brigade, first; 61st Battery, 14th Brigade, second.

19th MAY.—Sunday.—Voluntary Church Parade. Very hot.

20th MAY.—Monday.—Day spent in cleaning up generally. Exercise ride and grazing. Very hot.

21st MAY.—Tuesday.—Still very hot. Exercise ride and grazing. Orders to move to Berles. Aeroplane raid at night on aerodrome at Bruay.

22nd MAY.—Wednesday.—Left Divion at 7 a.m. and marched to Berles. Weather very hot. Stayed for the night at Berles.

23rd MAY.—Thursday.—Stayed for the day at Berles. Left Section moved on up into the Line and relieved part of 3rd Battery, C.F.A., at B.25 d 60.55 (Crater Position), pulling in our own guns. Weather has turned cold and windy. Section in charge of Lieut. Locke.

24th MAY.—Friday.—Balance of Battery left Berles at 9 a.m. for new Waggon Lines at L.12 a 50.90. A very unpleasant day, wet and windy. Reached lines shortly after noon. Major Greene and Lieut. Babbage, accompanied by Sgts. Wallas, Scougall, and Baillie, and Cpl. Weatherly and Gnr. Rennison, rode up to Main Position at A.30 c 29.29 at 2.30 p.m. The guns were pulled in without trouble the same evening. Waggon Lines at Anzin, a place which the Hun had registered exactly.

1918.

25th MAY.—Saturday.—Left Section heavily shelled from 5.30 to 6.50 p.m. after preliminary registration, lighter shelling starting at 3.30 p.m. No casualties. Some kit destroyed. Weather fine. About 400 rounds of 5.9's, 4.1's, and 77mm.'s fired at Left Section.

26th MAY.—Sunday.—Weather fine, but hazy. Guns at Main Position checked for line. Visibility only fair. Bdr. Hudson and working party of five reported.

27th MAY.—Monday.—Fine. Our vicinity shelled with gas from 2.30 a.m. to 4 a.m. Moved one gun from B.25 d 60.55 to B.26 d. 00.50.

28th MAY.—Tuesday.—O.C. went to Waggon Lines to see G.2 c Reserve Position.

29th MAY.—Wednesday.—Nothing very special. The O.C. up ahead looking over the defensive lines.

30th MAY.—Thursday.—Nothing eventful. This position is very quiet. The weather continues to be first class.

31st MAY.—Friday.—Weather warm and sunny. Visibility fairly good. Usual night harassing carried out.

1st JUNE.—Saturday.—Capt. Collinson went on Brigade Liaison duty. The Battery carried out support of a raid on our right by placing a dummy barrage in H.11 d at 12.35 a.m.; also fired slight retaliation at 2.15 a.m. Weather very fine, though somewhat hazy. New office completed and moved into. Work commenced on Gas Chamber for the use of men exposed to Mustard Gas.

1918.

2nd JUNE.—Sunday.—Our left forward shelled with gas from 2 a.m. to 3.30 a.m., and a considerable quantity drifted across our position. No casualties. During the morning the enemy strafed our Forward Section, Bdr. W. G. Chambers being wounded in the thigh from an air burst.

3rd JUNE.—Monday.—Quiet at the guns. In the evening four shells from a high-velocity gun dropped near our Waggon Lines. No damage done. Weather very fine.

4th JUNE.—Tuesday.—Our Waggon Lines moved to F.23 d 80.40. Weather continues fine. Gas Chamber finished. No. 5 gun moved to B.26 c 10.35. Our new Waggon Lines are on a hillside, close to two concrete gunpits in the valley.

5th JUNE.—Wednesday.—Quiet and uneventful. The Waggon Lines we vacated yesterday were shelled to-day, and the 66th Battery lost heavily and the 60th Battery slightly.

6th JUNE.—Thursday.—Very fine again. The Paymaster paid us a visit. Captain Collinson went to the Forward Section. Canadian mail in.

7th JUNE.—Friday.—Weather still very fine, but cloudy to-day. Quiet.

8th JUNE.—Saturday.—Weather still fine. Our Forward Section visited by the C.R.A. Quiet. The O.C. visited the Waggon Lines with his brother. Quite a strafe on our right about 10 p.m.

1918.

9th JUNE.—Sunday.—We were called on to answer S.Q.S. at 2.35 this morning. Expended 500 rounds. We came in for attention during the area shoot, which started at about 8 a.m. and kept up intermittently all morning and till about 1 p.m. J. C. Fry slightly wounded in the hand. No other casualties.

10th JUNE.—Monday.—Nothing very special. Brigade and the Heavy Battery close to them came in for a little attention towards the evening from the enemy. The feature of our present Battery Position is the "indoor" baseball, in which all ranks participate each evening.

11th JUNE.—Tuesday.—Quiet day also. Weather fine, with a fairly strong wind. Canadian mail in. The Major is away attending a Court of Enquiry.

12th JUNE.—Wednesday.—Another fine day. Quiet. The superiority of our airmen over the Hun on this sector is very noticeable at present. He rarely attempts to cross in daylight except in parties of five or six. Some of our men took part in a football match, 13th Brigade v. 14th Brigade.

13th JUNE.—Thursday.—Quiet. On the request of Brigade, Sergeant W. A. Wallas filled in application for temporary commission in the Canadian Field Artillery.

14th JUNE.—Friday.—Another quiet day. Strong wind blowing and dull intervals. At request of Brigade, Sergeant G. H. Scougall filled in application for temporary commission in Canadian Field Artillery.

15th JUNE.—Saturday.—Weather still windy and inclined to be cool. A few Whizz-bangs dropped in our vicinity about 9.50 p.m. Quiet.

1918.

16th JUNE.—Sunday.   Quiet.   Nothing of special importance.

17th JUNE.—Monday.—Fired at 1.30 this morning in support of raid on H.6 a 44.12—51.68.   Hauled Centre Section guns to a temporary position beside forward guns of Left Section.

18th JUNE.—Tuesday.—Balance of Battery moved forward to-night. Right Section guns being placed in a temporary position to the left front of Forward Section.   The Battery has moved forward to get within range to support a big raid on Newton Trench by the Scottish, 13th Battalion Royal Scots.

19th JUNE.—Wednesday.—A wettish day.   We do nothing to attract attention at present.

20th JUNE.—Thursday.—Nothing special.

21st JUNE.—Friday.—Early this morning we fired in support of the raid put on by the Scottish.   Report says that it was highly successful.   Moved four guns back to Main Position, leaving C and D Subs. forward.   A rainy evening.

22nd JUNE.—Saturday.—Full report of the raid received, in which the General pays the highest tribute to the artillery support.

23rd JUNE—Sunday.—Quiet day.   Weather fine.   Gnrs. Rennison and Howden left for Waggon Lines suffering from slight attack of "Spanish Influenza."   Observation good.

1918.

24th JUNE.—Monday.—Weather cloudy. Observation poor. Sgt. Scougall reported from Anti-Tank Gun. Rained from 5.30 to 6.30 p.m. Fired a barrage as "camouflage" at 11.30 p.m. No comeback. Quiet rest of night.

The following letter of appreciation was received from Lieut.-Col. J. A. Turner, Commanding the Battalion that conducted the raid :—

In the Field.

24th June, 1918.

DEAR GENERAL,—Many thanks for your note of congratulation.

It is to you that we are largely indebted for the success of the operation. The extreme accuracy of the barrage permitted some of the Battalion to get what would otherwise have been dangerously close to the enemy trenches.

During the practices I told the men that the Canadian gunners were behind us, and that they could rely on them.

After the show I talked to them regarding the barrage, and they all agreed that it was the best thing they had ever seen, and were greatly pleased.

Our casualties—27 in all—prove the excellency of the artillery programme. This is the first occasion on which I have personally had the co-operation of my countrymen, and I shall always remember it.

Yours sincerely,

J. A. TURNER, Lieut.-Col.

13th The Royal Scots.

58th Battery.
60th Battery.
61st Battery.
66th Battery.

14th Brigade, C.F.A.

T.1437.

26th June, 1918.

The above letter from Lieut.-Colonel J. A. Turner, Commanding 13th Battalion Royal Scots, to Brig.-Gen. W. O. H. Dodds, C.M.G., for your attention, please.

A. G. OLIVER, Lieut.

a/Adjutant, 14th Brigade, C.F.A.

25th JUNE.—Tuesday.—Weather in the morning fair and bright and up until 6 p.m., when it became dull and cloudy. Heinie had two balloons up all day. Sgt. J. A. Maclean proceeded "on command" to-day to attend Instructors' Signalling Course at Dunstable, England. Gunners Walshe and Jones A. sent down to Waggon Lines sick. A quiet day.

1918

26th JUNE.—Wednesday.—A few more cases to-day of the "flue." Nothing else of interest to report.

27th JUNE.—Thursday.—Sgt. Williams relieved Sgt. Link as Orderly Sergeant at the Main Position. Beautiful weather. Quiet day. A car of ammunition came in about 1.30 a.m.

28th JUNE.—Friday.—Sgt. Link, Gunners Ragotte and Hargrave, and Signaller Vallance went to the newly-established N.C.O.'s O.Pip this A.M. Quiet day. Fine weather.

29th JUNE.—Saturday.—About a dozen " 77's " paid the Main Position a call from 3.30 p.m. to 4 p.m. One landed close to the Signallers' sleeping quarters. A few, a little to our rear, burst on time. The balance fell to our left and rear and burst on percussion. Lieut. Virtue came from O.Pip and left for Waggon Lines this afternoon with a view to going on leave to-morrow. Had a " shoot " at 11.20 to-night. Fired 316 rounds. "B" Sub. Gun taken to I.O.M. at Louez to have Auxiliary Oil Tank fitted on, as well as the new Corrector for Muzzle Velocity. A beautiful day. Lieut. Raley returned from Brigade this evening.

30th JUNE.—Sunday.—Quiet.—Gunner Rennison reported back to the Gun Position. Weather fine.

1st JULY.—Monday.—Another very quiet day. Weather very fine. Some of the men at the Canadian Corps Sports at Tinques.

2nd JULY.—Tuesday.—Quiet. Weather fine, but cloudy towards evening. Major Greene returned to Battery Position and Capt. Collinson returned to Waggon Lines. Lieut. Locke reported to Battery Position and Lieut. Babbage went to Waggon Lines.

48

1918.

3rd JULY.—Wednesday.—About midnight last night, and again about 1.30 a.m. the enemy sent about 50 and 100 shells (5.9's) respectively into our area, wounding one man in 66th Battery. We suffered no casualties. Otherwise quiet.

4th JULY.—Thursday.—Nothing of special interest. Day rather cold.

5th JULY.—Friday.—Slightly warmer. Pay parade at the Guns. Enemy balloons up to-day for the first time for several days. Lieut. Raley returned from Forward and Lieut. Wildgoose went to O.Pip.

6th JULY.—Saturday.—Major Greene went to Brigade to act as C.O. during the absence, on leave, of Lieut.-Col. A. T. Ogilvie.

7th JULY.—Sunday.—Quiet. Nothing of importance. Weather fine.

8th JULY.—Monday.—Quiet. Weather warm and sultry. British Raid on our right at 9.50 p.m.

9th JULY.—Tuesday.—Nothing of any special importance.

10th JULY.—Wednesday.—Quiet again. Nothing doing. Weather fine. General Dodds inspected the Waggon Lines.

1918.

11th JULY.—Thursday.—Gunner Headrick, and Driver Fraser ordered to appear before the R.A.F. representative on 18th inst.

12th JULY.—Friday.—Quiet. Nothing important.

13th JULY.—Saturday.—Some Canadian mail in. Nothing special

14th JULY.—Sunday.—Nothing special. Some more Canadian mail in.

15th JULY.—Monday.—These days are very quiet. There is practically nothing doing except some construction work of one kind or another. We are building a second Gas Chamber at present.

16th JULY.—Tuesday.—Nothing of any particular importance. Indoor baseball still furnishes entertainment at the Battery Position during the evening.

17th JULY.—Wednesday.—Light shelling around us to-day. The shell used appears to be our own 18pdr. Weather fairly fine.

18th JULY.—Thursday.—Repetition of the shelling of yesterday. Several shrapnel shell burst round us while the ration waggon was being unloaded in the evening. No. 1 Gun was taken forward and put in No. 4 Pit and No. 3 Gun was brought back to the Main.

1918.

19th JULY.—Friday.—Nothing of special importance here. The latest unofficial French Report is that 22,000 prisoners and 300 guns have been captured in the attack that commenced two days ago, and that the advance has been 20 kilos. on a 40 kilo. front, between the Aisne and Marne.

20th JULY.—Saturday.—Rainstorm and thunder at 4.10 p.m. Lieut. Lowry arrived from 16th Battalion (Canadian Scottish) for instructional purposes. The entry entitling all men to wear Service Chevrons was made in the Paybooks during the Pay Parade on 18th.

21st JULY.—Sunday.—Nothing very special. A little gas over during the night

22nd JULY.—Monday.—Lieut. Raley proceeded on leave to England. The Brigade fired in support of a raid by the 102nd Battalion.

23rd JULY.—Tuesday.—Very wet and rainy and very windy. Some Canadian mail in. "C" Sub. Gun was returned from the Repair Shop and placed in action again.

24th JULY.—Wednesday.—Very uncertain weather at present. About thirty gas shells dropped in the vicinity of the position about 10.30 p.m.

25th JULY.—Thursday.—Calibration carried out. Lieut. Lowry (16th Battn.) was recalled to go on leave. A/B.S.M. Link paraded before the Air Board representative at Aubigny.

1918.

26th JULY.—Friday.—Cold. Very heavy showers. Fired at 8.55 p.m. in support of a raid, by laying down a "diversion" barrage. Gunner W. A. Headrick and Driver D. S. Fraser ordered to proceed to England on 29th as R.A.F. Cadets.

27th JULY.—Saturday.—Raining until noon. Nothing of much importance.

28th JULY.—Sunday.—Fairly fine all day but no brilliant sunshine. Visibility fair at times. At 11 p.m. we shot in support of a raid in B.24 a, B.24 c, B.24 b, and B.18c. Later we realised that all these raids were part of the splendidly conceived plan which resulted in the wonderful successes forward of Amiens.

29th JULY.—Monday.—Received "Warning Order" early this morning. Later we got orders to hand over to B Battery, 56th Brigade, R.F.A., relief to be completed by midnight 30th. Left Section was relieved and personnel returned to Waggon Lines Guns calibrated. Very warm, hazy day. This relief is not to be conducted in the manner general for some time. We are to take out our own guns and the relieving Battery is to place its guns in action.

30th JULY.—Tuesday.—Another very warm, hazy day. Handed the Main Position over to B/56, R.F.A., and our personnel all returned to the Waggon Lines.

31st JULY.—Wednesday.—The day (a very fine one) was spent in preparing to move. Unlike other occasions, the greatest secrecy as to our destination is being preserved. On other occasions very unwise information was made public regarding this matter.

1918.

1st AUGUST.—Thursday.—Reveille was at 1 a.m., and we marched shortly after 2 a.m. for Aubigny, where we entrained and left about 11.2 a.m., having had breakfast at Aubigny. About 5 p.m. we detrained at Bacouel and marched at 8.15 p.m. to Boutillerie, reaching there about 1 a.m. on the morning of August 2nd.

2nd AUGUST.—Friday.—We finally got stowed away about 2 a.m. this morning. The Waggon Lines are in a field near the Chateau and the old Munition Works. No move was made, and the day, which was showery, was spent in resting and cleaning up generally. The map location of the Horse Lines is M. 27 c 80.10.

3rd AUGUST.—Saturday.—Another somewhat showery day. In the evening we moved again, from Billets No. 35 and 45 to Nos. 29, 39, 41, 43, 45, 47 and 9, with Horse Lines at M.33 b 90.90. These horse lines are down under trees on very swampy ground. Ammunition went up by pack horse to-night to dump at O.34 c 40.50.

4th AUGUST.—Sunday.—Church Parade at 2.30 p.m. Showery weather. We are spending our nights now in all-night journeys to the front line area with ammunition for an intended " shoot." Just below our kitchen a great number of Tanks are concealed under the trees overhanging the road. They are "double-banked" and must extend for fully four hundred yards, closely packed. They are also covered with camouflage.

5th AUGUST.—Monday.—Very wet and rainy. The B.C., Captain, and Signalling Sergeant (A/Sgt. C. A. Bryant) out all day on reconnaissance. Major Greene returned from First Army Artillery School. Four guns were taken in to-night and camouflaged.

1918.

6th AUGUST.—Tuesday.—Weather showery. The remaining two
guns went in to-night and skeleton detachments. Sgt. N.
Link received orders to proceed to England for Cadet course
in the R.A.F. Sgt. W. A. Wallas, being Senior Sergeant,
took over the duties of Sgt.-Major.

7th AUGUST.—Wednesday.—Sgt. N. Link, who has been acting as
Battery Sgt.-Major, left for England this morning. The
balance of the Gun detachment, plus the Signallers and
specialists necessary, under Lieut. Wildgoose, marched up
to the Gun position in the evening. It was a very hot
journey. As soon as everything was in order the men went
to work digging "funk-pits," an operation that was fre-
quently interrupted by the Hun harassing fire. We were
well within machine-gun range, and the enemy impressed
that fact on us during the night.

8th AUGUST.—Thursday.—The Battery took part in the offensive
started on the Amiens front to-day. Zero hour was at
4.20 a.m. The Battery Position was in a field of ripe wheat
at U.3 d 54.64 (Demuin), to the right of the village of
Villers Brettonneux. Starting at Zero we fired for two hours
and twenty-eight minutes, our range opening at 1,200 yards
and lifting, in 100 yard lifts, to 5,500 yards. We expended
nearly 2,000 rounds on the Barrage. Before our barrage was
finished we could see the Royal Horse Artillery and the
Cavalry moving up on either side of us. The attack was
supported by a considerable number of Tanks, and there
was no preparatory bombardment. Later in the day our
Waggon Lines were moved to a position between Lama and
Leopard Woods. The enemy's bombing 'planes were very
active during the night. During the Barrage one lone
Fritz shell, a "77," landed in the ammunition about five
feet from B Sub. pit, missing Lieut. Virtue's head by about
ten inches. Luckily, the shell was a "dud," or we would
have had a considerable addition to our Casualty List. The
force of the impact smashed a couple of our shells into
several pieces. At the conclusion of the Barrage the Battery
went into Reserve.

9th AUGUST.—Friday.—Stayed in Waggon Lines. More bombing
during the night.

1918.

10th AUGUST.—Saturday.—At 5 a.m. we received orders to move, and we moved at 7 a.m. Route via Ignacourt—Cayeux-en-Santerre to rendezvous at Beaufort, arriving at noon. Went into action at 6 p.m. at L. 14 c. 05.05—alongside a trench in front of Folies. Shooting on Fouquescourt. Major T. D. J. Ringwood, O.C. 60th Battery, was killed instantly to-day whilst on reconnaissance.

11th AUGUST.—Sunday.—From 9.30 a.m. to 10.48 a.m. we barraged the Hun between Fouquescourt and Parvillers.

12th AUGUST.—Monday.—Weather fine and hot. Considerable artillery activity. We fired on La Chavette. Lieut. Raley liaising with 42nd Battalion, who relieved the Border Regiment. P.P.C.L.I. on our right from Parvillers south. Lieut Wildgoose at O.Pip. During the night of 12th/13th the Hun put on a fairly heavy Area Shoot on the Forward and Support Areas, causing all lines of communication with Artillery to be broken. Signaller W. C. MacNeill, showing extreme devotion to duty, kept up communication between Infantry and Artillery Brigade throughout the "strafe." The highest praise is due to this signaller for his work on this occasion—work performed under heavy shell fire and alone—and it is hoped that the authorities will see fit to give suitable recognition.

13th AUGUST.—Tuesday.—The 66th Battery and ourselves changed positions this evening. A scorching day. Fairly quiet. The Y.M.C.A. established a canteen in the village to our left (Rouvroy) either yesterday or this morning. It is a most unhealthy locality. The Hun appears to be suspicious of the place, for he shelled it spasmodically all morning.

14th AUGUST.—Wednesday.—Considerable amount of harassing fire by enemy on forward areas. We saw several air fights during the day. The Hun treated us to a dose of gas during the night (14th), and as there was no wind and our position is in a valley it did not clear very quickly.

1918.

15th AUGUST.—Thursday.—Some light harassing fire on the support area in front of us during the day. The waggon line area around Folies bombed at night. Fired on La Chavette, and our people took it after a concentrated bombardment.

16th AUGUST.—Friday.—The enemy apparently is paying a good deal of attention to night bombing, with the hope of harassing our transport lines. Moved forward about 1,000 yards. Several S.O.S. calls. At 6 p.m. we were ordered to move and moved at 7 p.m. Our new location is L.21 A.05.45.

17th AUGUST.—Saturday.—The weather is cooler to-day and the sky cloudy to-night. Much less bombing of our lines to-night. Weather fine. O.C. liaised with 3rd Can. Inf. Brigade under General Tunford. Fairly quiet on our front, though there was much firing on our right on the Fresnoy area. Our wire stopped on a line Salmon—Oberon Trenches.

18th AUGUST.—Sunday.—Started showery, but cleared up with a strong west wind. O.C. and Lieut. Raley reconnoitred position near Fonquescourt.

19th AUGUST.—Monday.—Moved Waggon Lines from near Folies to position at L.13 d 40.70, slightly in rear of our old Battery Position. The drawback to horse lines here is the watering question, as horses have to be watered at Folies. More reconnaissance made in the Fouquescourt Area. We have orders for a tentative move. Lieut. Raley at O.Pip.

20th AUGUST.—Tuesday.—Weather warmer. Overcast, but not wet. Lieut. Virtue returned from liaison with 13th Battalion. Major Ewing, of the 42nd Battalion, wrote a note mentioning Lieut. Raley for good liaison work. Signaller McNeill, W. C.'s, name gone in for repairing lines. Lieut. Wildgoose at O.P. The previous evening the enemy threw over quite a bit of harassing fire and blew in the Officers' Mess in the trench.

1918.

21st AUGUST.—Wednesday.—Weather turned very hot again. In the evening the guns were taken out of action. All ammunition (except Echelon) was returned to Dump, and the Battery marched to its old Waggon Lines at Llama Wood, having travelled all night. Bright moonlight night. The recaptured area seems to be in a very unsanitary condition. Many dead horses were scattered over that part through which our route lay, and the odour was disgusting.

22nd AUGUST.—Thursday.—Rested in Waggon Lines during the day and marched again at 8.50 p.m. Marched all night. Got a new gun for "D" Sub.

23rd AUGUST.—Friday.—Arrived at Saleux (Pont de Metz) at 3 a.m. and rested here for the remainder of the day. Good water for the horses. Many of the men had an open-air bath in the stream.

24th AUGUST.—Saturday.—Moved off from lines in Saleux at 2.30 p.m. and finally entrained about 6 p.m. after a long wait. Loading facilities at this point are very primitive.

25th AUGUST.—Sunday.—Arrived at Aubigny about 6 a.m., being delayed two hours at St. Pol owing to enemy bombing activity. Had breakfast and marched by sections to Waggon Lines at L.18 c, near Arras. Preparations made to go into action very early to-morrow morning.

1918.

26th AUGUST.—Monday.—Guns, firing battery, and first-line waggons moved off from lines at 1 a.m. and moved up to a position of readiness at H.25 a. On this occasion we do not fire in the barrage, but move forward as the attacking infantry advance. The guns were placed in position at H.33 b, and while the limbers were still on the ground Sgt. Williams and Gnr. Milne were wounded. It is believed that one of the horses kicked a bomb of some description. During the day the Waggon Lines were moved to G.30 b, near Cemetery Track. The attack opened at 3 a.m. on Monchy Hill, the barrage lasting to 6.28 a.m. 3rd Division North, 2nd Division South of Cambrai Road. We were held in mobile reserve, moving forward at 7 a.m. in support of 8th C.I.B. Objectives were quickly taken, casualties few. Monchy was in our hands by noon. Beyond that the situation was obscure. During the evening our S.O.S. Lines covered Pelves. It rained slightly. Right Section took up forward position north of Scarpe in afternoon.

27th AUGUST.—Tuesday.—Very rainy and uncertain. We fired on Barrage about 5 a.m. Lieut. Virtue moved the Right Section up on the left front near the Scarpe, covering the P.P.C.L.I. yesterday afternoon. Lieuts. Wildgoose and Richer and S./M. Wallas went up behind Monchy and chose a position in case of a move. We are keeping about 200 rounds of ammunition per gun. The 51st Division on our left, north of the Scarpe, took Mount Pleasant Wood. Gnr. Belford, "F" Sub. was wounded by a backfire. Gun was sent to the I.O.M. Gnr. A. Clifford was also burned.

28th AUGUST.—Wednesday.—Last night we got an order to move forward and we moved to the crest of Orange Ridge after considerable difficulty as it was very dark and the ground covered with wire, shell holes, and old trenches. Weather wet at times with a strong wind. From 11 to 12 noon we fired to support an attack by the 9th Can. Inf. Brigade, who took Boiry. This apparently outflanked Jigsaw Wood, to which the Infantry on our front advanced in the afternoon and took it. A few H.V. shells fell round the position. No damage.

1918.

29th AUGUST.—Thursday.—Fine day. The O.C. and Lieut Locke reconnoitred Boiry and the Guemappe Valley. Our Infantry took Remy, and the Bosche is apparently just sitting down into his Drocourt-Queant Line. North of the Scarpe, Greenland Hill was taken to-day, so we were able to advance the Battery down the valley of the Scarpe to H.30 b 5.7. We had a quiet evening. Our Waggon Lines moved to H.27, on the top of the rise, and about 2,500 yards further on.

30th AUGUST.—Friday.—A dull day. Wind from west. Capt. Collinson and Lieuts. Locke and Virtue went South on a mounted reconnaissance near Remy, and coincided with a whizz-bang bombardment of one of our Battery positions. In the race which followed Capt. Collinson is said to have been a good first—weights conceded. In the afternoon we got orders to move 450 rounds per gun to a battle position south of Boiry. O.C. and Lieut. Locke went up and chose a position. Ammunition drawn up in the evening. Quite a lot of harassing fire on both sides. Enemy aeroplanes did a bit of bombing. The Infantry that we have been covering have made many changes the last few days, and it is difficult to follow who is in the Line ahead of us, one of the units being a composite Brigade of Imperial M.M.G.'s and Canadian Cyclist Corps—about their first time in the Line, apparently thrown in for an emergency. Gnr. Selvage, G. H., wounded by a single bomb dropped by an enemy 'plane about fifty yards from the position. A wonder that there were not more casualties, as the Mulligan was then being served.

31st AUGUST.—Sunday.—A dull day. Some R.F.A. pulled in, in column of bunches, and of course drew some shell-fire on us as well as themselves. Lieuts. Locke and Babbage took forward "C," "D," and "E" Guns to near Boiry and the remainder of the ammunition. This afternoon we moved our Waggon Lines to H.24 c, just behind the main Battery in the Scarpe Valley, and had a very unpleasant time. As far as one could judge we were under observation from the ground, and we had barely got the horses on the Lines before the Hun opened up on us with four guns, apparently a 4.2 Howitzer Battery. After giving us a warm twenty minutes he stopped and we pulled out as fast as possible. Casualties one horse and one mule killed and one man shell-shocked. We have a big horse-shoe round us. If he had put over air bursts or used instantaneous fuse we would have been out of luck.

1918.

1st SEPTEMBER.—Sunday.—The other two guns went forward in the evening. A fair amount of harassing fire. Brigade Headquarters is in rear of Boiry. The night was fairly decent but we did not get an hour's sleep. Dvr. R. Heatherton was wounded to-day at the Waggon Lines at H.27, as he then put over a number of air bursts while we were enjoying breakfast (bacon and bread). Gnr. Powell and Dvr. Kilgour were hit with small splinters at the same time, but in neither case did they penetrate the skin. Dvr. Connolly was also hit in the back and the skin bruised.

2nd SEPTEMBER.—Monday.—The Canadians again attacked early this morning at 5 a.m., and according to the newspaper report "burst the Hindenburg Line," breaking through the Wotan Switch Line. While moving our guns forward through the village of Vis-en-Artois we had the misfortune to have Lieut. C. E. M. Richer, A./B.S.M. Wallas, and Dvr. Owens wounded, the first two very seriously. Later in the day Cpl. Clapstone and Gnr. Kinsey were wounded, the former severely. Our Waggon Lines were moved to N.10 b0.5, near an old trench. From 5 until about 8 a.m. we fired in the barrage covering Dury. Apparently things went very well with our infantry, as they walked over their objectives, passing through the Drocourt-Queant Line, and going over Dury Hill without a hitch and fairly few casualties. At 9 a.m. D and E Subs. went forward to support the 10th Can. Inf. Brigade. The situation is very obscure. The 10th C.I.B. did not know just where their units were and the enemy artillery was very heavy, coming from Ecourt-St. Quentin, and enfilade from north of the Scarpe. This Section came into action in P.25 b and was soon after joined by the remaining three guns, which had experienced some casualties en route. During the day we were continually harassed by a 4.1 Section in enfilade. We held the air in the morning, but in the afternoon the enemy seemed to do as he pleased, coming over in swarms, twenty coming over at a time. We had rather a poor night of it, between shell holes, harassing fire, and the rain, but our shell holes, though cold, were not inundated.

1918.

3rd SEPTEMBER.—Tuesday.—Reconnaissance was made by the
O.C. and Lieut. Wildgoose, and a forward position was
chosen beside Dury at P.21 c 60.10. The Battery moved
up here in the evening under Capt. Collinson, who relieved
the O.C. A./Bdr. Lyons was wounded to-day. We received
word to-day that Lieut. C. E. M. Richer died to-day of
wounds received yesterday. He was buried on the 4th in
Ligny St. Flochel, Map 51 C. b 6 d 40, Plot 3, Row D.,
Grave 25. Our Waggon Lines moved to Cherisy on the rise
east of the village. Considerable bombing that night. The
Hun also put two or three High Velocity near the road
below the village.

4th SEPTEMBER.—Wednesday.—Nothing of any particular importance. The gun position is alongside a trench which
formed part of the Hindenburg Line, just behind and west
of Dury. The men live in the trench. Alongside us is a
battery of South African Heavy Artillery.

5th SEPTEMBER.—Thursday.—Nothing of special interest. A most
beautiful day as far as the weather is concerned. The Centre
Section moved forward before dawn to-day to a position in
25 a, between Saudemont and Ecourt-St. Quentin, Lieut.
R. H. Babbage in charge. Considerable harassing fire in
the vicinity of Dury.

6th SEPTEMBER.—Friday.—Fairly quiet. Prepared to move the
remaining two guns forward. We experienced a torrential
fall of rain in the afternoon, which caused the collapse of
nearly all the bivouacs in the trench and flooded the dug-
out in which the officers are living. No. 5 gun moved forward this morning. Gnr. W. Colchester wounded to-day.

7th SEPTEMBER.—Saturday.—Moved forward in front of Dury
early this morning while it was still dark, and placed the
guns in position in a trench behind Recourt. Officers and
men are living in rough "bivvies" in the trench, which is
a poor one and very shallow in places. The enemy shelled
the area persistently during the day and we had to keep
to our trench to avoid casualties. We are relieved *in situ*
by the B.293 R.A.F. during the day, and all personnel returned to the Waggon Lines.

1918.

8th SEPTEMBER.—Sunday.—We took over five guns from B. 293 late last night and placed them in our old position in rear of Dury early this morning. In afternoon we were ordered to send up three men per gun and two officers to man guns, although they were then miles out of range, but well within range of Hun guns firing from north of the Scarpe. Lieuts. Locke and Virtue went up in charge.

9th SEPTEMBER.—Monday.—Weather very rainy and very windy. We regret to record that we have received advice that Sgt. (A./B.S.M.) Wallas died of wounds received on the 2nd, and that Cpl. Clapstone has also died. They are both buried in Fambourg Cemetery, Arras.

10th SEPTEMBER.—Tuesday.—Weather poor. Rainy and uncertain. Decidedly cold.

11th SEPTEMBER.—Wednesday.—Another poor day. Wet and windy. Bathing parade for the Battery to Rohart Factory, on the Cambrai Road. An unhealthy bath-house as the Bosche bumps the odd H.V. shell in round that locality.

12th SEPTEMBER.—Thursday.—Still at Cherisy. Weather wet and stormy.

13th SEPTEMBER.—Friday.—Nothing special to-day. Very heavy wind and rain accompanied by thunder last night, with the result that many of the "bivvies" were blown down and nearly everyone flooded out.

14th SEPTEMBER.—Saturday.—Nothing of particular importance. Still marking time at Cherisy, with our guns in reserve (in position, but out of range and silent) alongside the trench behind Dury. Weather better to-day.

1918.

15th SEPTEMBER.—Sunday.—Nothing very special.

16th SEPTEMBER.—Monday.—We were instructed to submit names for ordinary leave to the United Kingdom. So far the only man granted ordinary leave to the United Kingdom is Gnr. Powell, who drew first place.

17th SEPTEMBER.—Tuesday.—Nothing very special. There is some idea that we may go out on rest.

18th SEPTEMBER.—Wednesday.—Moved the Waggon Lines from in front of Cherisy to N.W. of Wancourt. Six guns still in reserve at Dury, under Lieuts. Virtue and Raley. The O.C. returned to-day. The weather is excellent.

19th SEPTEMBER.—Thursday.—Weather windy, but fair. Made some new N.C.O.'s. The Sgts. now are :—A./B.S.M. Scougall, G. H.; "A" Sub., Weatherley, G. W.; "B" Sub.; Belingham, A. B.; "C" Sub., Wray, C. F.; "D" Sub., Baillie, J. B.; "E" Sub., Douglass, L. V.; "F" Sub., Williams, W. B.; "H.Q.," Bryant, C. A. Leave started for the men to-day. Teams made a trip to take out the guns. This was cancelled later.

20th SEPTEMBER.—Friday.—Turned a bit cold during the night and rained off and on during the day. Wind from the west. Hauled out guns to-night.

21st SEPTEMBER.—Saturday.—Not a bad day on the whole. Rained a couple of times but the sun soon dried things up. During the day we moved Waggon Lines to Hendicourt, V.6 d 8.4. The O.C. and Lieut. Locke reconnoitred a Battery Position in D.6 b 3.6, west of Inchy. The other batteries in the Brigade are close by. It is rather a desolate rolling country and the position is near Inchy and the Canal du Nord, which is at present dry. The position is one to be used during the capture of Bourlon Village and Wood—the only obstacles this side of Cambrai. We are right beside the Hindenburg Line with its many rows of well-constructed barbed wire.

1918.

22nd SEPTEMBER.—Sunday.—Rained off and on. Officers and N.C.O.'s reconnoitred the routes to Battery Position. In the evening Lieuts. Locke and Virtue went forward with 72 pack horses and six waggons of the 2nd Section, D.A.C., under Lieut. McNab. The pack horses made three trips altogether, including one to Cagnicourt, taking in 2,500 rounds altogether. They left at 6 p.m. and got back at 6 a.m.—twelve hours' heavy work. After midnight it became clear moonlight, and fortunately the enemy harassing fire was not too heavy. The men and teams worked well.

23rd SEPTEMBER.—Monday.—A cold day with a few showers, but the odd bit of sunshine left things fairly dry underfoot. The O.C. went to Brigade as the C.O. has gone to Divarty, *re* the General gone to the 11th Division (Imperial). The remaining 2,000 for the show were taken in to-night under Lieuts. Raley and Babbage. We sent up a Working Party to the position this morning to prepare platforms for guns.

24th SEPTEMBER.—Tuesday.—Moved our lines to-day to V.28 d 8.7, in front of Bullecourt.

25th SEPTEMBER.—Wednesday.—Rained a bit and then cleared up, ending a fine day. Received the maps and "dope" for the "Show." Moved the Right Section guns into position.

26th SEPTEMBER.—Thursday. Fine day. Remainder of the guns and the personnel moved into the Battery Position in the evening.

1918.

27th SEPTEMBER.—Friday.—At 5.20 a.m. we commenced firing on the Barrage, which lasted till 11.20, during which time we supported the 1st Divisional Infantry, and at the completion of which we were transferred to the 3rd Division. Everything went as per schedule, the Infantry crossing the Canal rapidly and with small loss, taking Bourlon Village and Wood about noon. The left of the attack, including the 11th Imperial Division, swinging north, and in a turning movement cutting off the heights of Oisy le Verger, thus extending our left flank to the river on the north. In the afternoon the Battery crossed the Canal by "A" Track between 3 and 4 p.m., taking up a position east of the Canal, moving at midnight to a position west of Bourlon Village. The move, conducted in the dark and without previous reconnaissance, was most difficult, and the extreme darkness of the night added to the difficulty. Cpl. McNeill was wounded severely in the arm during the enemy retaliation, and the Battery was extremely lucky in avoiding heavier casualties—thanks to the pits dug by the working parties. We fired about 2,300 rounds.

28th SEPTEMBER.—Saturday.—From 6 to 8 a.m. we fired on a Barrage covering from Bourlon Wood out to the Marcoing Line. Things went well, evidently taking the enemy by surprise, and anticipating a counter-attack of his to cover Cambrai. The day started cold and wet but cleared up later. In the evening we moved up to the N.E. Corner of Bourlon Wood. This afternoon Capt. Collinson and Lieut. Virtue rode forward on a reconnaissance. They were obliged to leave their horses and go on foot. They found our Infantry held up near St. Olle and rather badly broken up, owing to stubborn defence and heavy machine-gun fire.

29th SEPTEMBER.—Sunday.—At 8 a.m. we fired a Creeping Barrage covering St. Olle, but the enemy put up a stubborn resistance and the advance was slow and costly. We were covering the 2nd C.M.R.'s of the 8th Canadian Inf. Brigade. It turned out a fine day.

30th SEPTEMBER.—Monday.—A dull day. We moved last night about a thousand yards forward. Kept plugging at the Hun in front of Cambrai, in conjunction with a show on our left. On our right they appear to have crossed the Canal and are working in south of Cambrai.

1918.

1st OCTOBER.—Tuesday.—We shot on a Barrage to assist 1st, 3rd, and 4th Divisions take the high ground N.W. of Cambrai and seize the bridgeheads over the Canal de l'Escault. The Bosche fought stubbornly, and after taking Tilloy and Cuvillers, our left had to retire from the high ground round the latter place owing to the 11th Division (further left) failing to hold Blecourt and Avincourt.

2nd OCTOBER.—Wednesday.—Quite a decent day. The Bosche counter-attacked heavily in front of Cuvillers, but made no progress.

3rd OCTOBER.—Thursday.—Fine weather continues. Much aerial activity. Sgt. Charles Frederick Wray and Gnr. Robert Watson received the award of the Military Medal.

4th OCTOBER.—Friday.—Things fairly quiet.

5th OCTOBER.—Saturday.—A fairly decent day. Some shelling and bombing last night. We took over from the A. 186 and the Right Section moved to X.8 b 6.4, changing places. Capt. Collinson reconnoitred the place. The position is near Haynecourt.

6th OCTOBER.—Sunday.—The remaining four guns and personnel moved to new position. We are behind the 34th Infantry Brigade (Imperial), General Clay in command. They consist of the Manchesters, Dorsets, and Northumberland Fusiliers. We are firing on the south of Abencourt.

7th OCTOBER.—Monday.—Very quiet. Fairly cold. About 11 p.m. the Hun came over and dropped four bombs on the Battery Position and many in the valley in rear. No casualties.

1918.

8th OCTOBER.—Tuesday. Rained a bit last night, but not bad this morning. At 4.30 a.m. we shot on Abencourt to assist the Infantry in a raid, lasting for two hours.

9th OCTOBER.—Wednesday.—Quite a fine day. The 2nd Division went forward and took Ramillies and Eswars, outflanking the Bosche at Cuvillers and Paillencourt, by working up the Canal towards Estrun. This is in conjunction with the big attack which enveloped Cambrai, ultimately penetrating to Le Chateau. Unfortunately the Imperial Infantry on our immediate front allowed the Hun to retire at his leisure over the river. In the afternoon the Battery moved position to due west of Sancourt to X. 12 c 10.90, but the enemy got well out of range.

10th OCTOBER.—Thursday.—Fairly decent day. The Battery moved up to Eswars and the Waggon Lines a mile behind at X. 12 c 10.70. The guns are at S.12 d 60.40. While the Waggon Lines were changing Gnr. J. C. Waldie was accidentally wounded in the arm by the explosion of a bomb that was detonated by a waggon driving over it. A couple of horses were wounded at the same time.

11th OCTOBER.—Friday.—A wet day. Nothing doing.

12th OCTOBER.—Saturday.—A dull day. Our position in a big field of cabbages and turnips. No civilians around here.

13th OCTOBER.—Sunday.—Another dull day. The O.C. returned from Brigade. The guns moved to a position in front of Thun Leveque. In the morning our Waggon Lines moved from Sancourt and we camped in an open field about four miles farther on and towards Tilloy. The enemy apparently spotted us from a slag heap, as he sent over several shells, a couple of which landed in our lines without doing any damage. We left as soon as possible and made lines just on the left of Ramillies. We had to cross a ridge to get to this position and the Hun spotted us again and let us have a few more rounds, but none of them came near enough to disturb us.

1918.

14th OCTOBER.—Monday.—Moved No. 4 gun forward to position by the Canal lock. O.Pipped from Caesar's Camp and had some good sniping at the enemy across the valley.

15th OCTOBER.—Tuesday.—A dull, but typical Fall day. We are now supporting the 19th Battalion. 27th on the left and 18th on the right, of the 4th Canadian Infantry Brigade.

16th OCTOBER.—Wednesday.—A wet night and a drizzly day. Poor visibility. Capt. Collinson left to take over command of 32nd Battery, 8th Army Brigade. Men and horses are pretty tired, and a rest would be appreciated.

17th OCTOBER.—Thursday.—Another dull day. Quiet night. "C" Sub. joined "D" Sub. forward, taking Lieut. Raley with them. We hear Douai and Lille have been taken.

18th OCTOBER.—Friday.—Another misty day. Fairly quiet. The 2nd Division crossed the river during the night and now hold Wasnaubac and Wavrichain, and are advancing east along the north of the river, linking up with the 1st Division on the left. In the late afternoon the Battery moved forward to Paillencourt, the O.C. again going to Brigade. Lieut. Mackenzie, R. C., joined us to-day. During the harassing fire which we carried out during the night Gnr. H. A. Murchie was badly burned by a backfire of the gun and was evacuated.

19th OCTOBER.—Saturday.—During the evening we moved from Paillencourt to Marquette, a rather unpleasant trip. However, we got fairly comfortable quarters.

1918.

20th OCTOBER.—Sunday.—Went forward to Rouelx and took up a position there in a field of turnips. The day was wet but cleared up later. It was at Rouelx that we first met liberated civilians in any numbers, and their joy at the departure of the Huns was unbounded. French flags hung everywhere. The Curé (Parish Priest) had hidden when the Germans left and was greatly delighted with his escape. He shook hands with us and took off his Biretta to us when leaving. About the first thing we laid eyes on while marching to Rouelx in the morning was a McCormick Binder. It looked rather out of place. After dinner we moved on to Escaudin, where we all got into comfortable billets. There the civilians also gave us a good welcome. They related how the Germans had stolen everything of value, even down to the wool stuffing of their mattresses.

21st OCTOBER.—Monday.—We spent the morning in Escaudin, and after dinner moved on to a small village on the outskirts of Haveluy. We are now back in the mining district, with slag heaps all round us. The guns were placed in action, or rather placed in position for action if necessary, as we are in Divisional Reserve. To-day A./B.S.M. Scougall, Sgt. Baillie, Sgt. Douglass, and A./Sgt. Bryant were interviewed by G.O.C., R.A., Canadian Corps, with a view to being granted commissions in the C.F.A.

22nd OCTOBER.—Tuesday.—Nothing very special. In Divisional Reserve. Horses a bit thin and haggard looking, but haven't lost a single one.

23rd OCTOBER.—Wednesday.—A fine day. Still in Divisional Reserve. We got a few shells round the vicinity of our billets in the morning, and Cpl. G. G. Neher received a slight scratch in the leg from a splinter. Capt. C. King reported for duty from the 66th Battery, and Lieut. Mackenzie reported back to 66th Battery. Capt. King is vice Capt. C. H. Collinson, promoted Major and transferred to 32nd Battery. Lieut. C. H. Locke returned from leave to the United Kingdom.

24th OCTOBER.—Thursday.—A fine day for this time of year. Still in same place. The O.C., Major Greene, left to-day on leave to the United Kingdom.

1918.

25th OCTOBER.—Friday.—A fair day. One man per subsection returned to the Waggon Lines, as we are still in reserve and nothing much to do.

26th OCTOBER.—Saturday.—Misty in the morning, but developed into a bright, sunny day. At 10 a.m. this morning our guns opened up on the front facing us, but as we are not in action we do not know what is happening. The Bosche treated us to a few rounds of harassing fire at night, the shells landing a couple of hundred yards away from us.

27th OCTOBER.—Sunday.—Nothing special to-day. The weather is good. A little aerial activity to-day. The enemy had a couple of 'planes over.

28th OCTOBER.—Monday.—Another fine day. In the evening we moved to a position in the rear of a farmhouse (Urtebise Farm). The programme was a "show" in the morning, but after we got into position our move was cancelled and we were ordered to remain "silent" and to keep under cover, with the guns well camouflaged.

29th OCTOBER.—Tuesday.—The guns were dug in and well camouflaged before the morning mist dispersed. The day turned out an excellent one. The enemy made things lively in our vicinity during the a.m. at odd intervals, putting salvoes of 5.9's over. Orders were received to put 2,400 rounds of ammunition at La Sentinel, and accordingly 1,056 rounds were hauled from here, together with 500 rounds from our Echelon. The dump will be completed to-morrow evening by the hauling of another 900. Orders at present call for everything to be ready at Midnight to-morrow. Lieut. Raley went to Brigade to act as Adjutant. Dvr. St. Ours was wounded in the shoulder this evening, but remained on duty.

30th OCTOBER.—Wednesday.—A fine sunny day. Slight wind. Further orders received to-day amend things somewhat. The ammunition goes in to-night but the guns do not move to-night as arranged. We put over 100 rounds of harassing fire on the Hun during the afternoon, together with a further 50 rounds during the night.

31st OCTOBER.—Thursday.—Weather fine but dull. In the evening we moved from Urtebise Farm, taking up a position at La Sentinel (Map location, D.11 d 80.20). The men are living behind the knoll to the flank of the Battery and slightly in rear. Orders arrived during the late evening for a "show" to-morrow.

1st NOVEMBER.—Friday.—At a Zero hour of 5,15 a.m., in darkness and a thick cold mist, we joined in an intense Barrage in support of an attack by the Fourth Division on Mont Huoy, south of Valenciennes, which culminated in the capture of Valenciennes itself. Our Barrage on this occasion was enfilade and was laid down 500 yards in advance of the main creeping barrage. The weather became fine and sunny during the forenoon. From the O.Pip huge columns of smoke could be seen rising from a number of points in Valenciennes, which had been fired by the Hun. In the afternoon we were placed under tactical control of 52nd Battery, C.F.A., for close support of a Battalion of 4th Division. The 60th Battery on our right rear received a severe drubbing. Lieut. Staunton rejoined the Battery in the early morning.

2nd NOVEMBER.—Saturday.—A quiet day. We did not fire. The weather was dull and overcast, with rain at times. A marked contrast to yesterday. Lieut. R. H. Babbage has been awarded the Military Cross.

3rd NOVEMBER.—Sunday.—We moved in the morning and placed the Guns in position along the Canal Bank at Valenciennes. We did not fire in this position and moved at night to a position at E.4 d 60.45, on the outskirts of Valenciennes. The Hun has played tricks with the Canal, and as a result, while passing through Valenciennes, we had to pass through several streets that were flooded to a depth of eighteen inches.

4th NOVEMBER.—Monday.—Moved the Left Section forward to W.30 d 30.30, along the Mons Road beside a Chateau at St. Saule. Nothing special. We expected to move forward, but no orders arrived so we went to bed in hopes——

1918.

5th NOVEMBER.—Tuesday.—Orders arrived to move forward and we moved at 2 a.m. to a position alongside the two forward Guns. At 5.30 a.m. we fired a Barrage for one hour. Considering the short notice both the move and the Barrage were carried out in a manner reflecting great credit on everyone. The day settled down into a very wet one. At 10.30 p.m. we moved up the Mons Road to a position on the outskirts of Onnaing. The enemy was more energetic with harassing fire than has been the case just lately, and Signaller K. G. McTeer was slightly wounded from a shell that burst almost on the hard road. "Stout" was evacuated to the Dressing Station.

6th NOVEMBER.—Wednesday.—At 5.30 a.m. we barraged for 116 minutes, lifting from 2,400 yards to 5,400 yards. The Barrage partly covered Quievrain, in Belgium. The enemy showed great activity last night and early this morning. He harassed our position continually, and only the state of the ground (which was soft mud) and our usual luck saved us from heavy casualties. The day was very wet. Quite a number of prisoners came down.

7th NOVEMBER.—Thursday.—Moved back to Waggon Lines in St. Saule. We are now in Corps Reserve. The weather is rainy and rather miserable. As we expect to be out for possibly a week or more, every effort will be made to clean up and re-equip.

8th NOVEMBER.—Friday.—Rather uncertain weather. Rainy at times. Everyone working hard to clean up the guns and vehicles.

9th NOVEMBER.—Saturday.—Left our Waggon Lines in St. Saule this morning and moved to new Waggon Lines in Quievrain in Belgium. We were to go into action to-night and fire in the morning, but this was cancelled as the Hun evacuated the ground over which we were to fire. Just before we entered Quievrain a squadron of the Fifth Lancers, accompanied by two sections of Royal Horse Artillery, passed us —moving up into action.

1918.

10th NOVEMBER.—Sunday.—Matters rather uncertain to-day. We left Quievrain in the afternoon and moved on to Thulin. Weather fine but rather cold. Particulars as to how we are billeted are recorded under date of 11th inst.

11th NOVEMBER.—Monday.—Weather fine and cold. Billets in Thulin : Officers' Mess in Mill owner's residence. Office and Q.M. Stores in Manager's residence. N.C.O.'s and men in Workmen's houses. Stables in the Factory. Gun Park in Factory Yard. The Armistice began at 11 a.m. to-day, 11th Nov.—i.e., 11th hour, 11th day, 11th month. The news was announced by Lieut. R. Wildgoose at the Dinner hour. It was taken very quietly by the troops. Half holiday and rum issue.

12th NOVEMBER.—Tuesday.—Weather fine and bright. Reveille 6 a.m. Cleaning up. Lines properly located and Gun Park lined up.

13th NOVEMBER.—Wednesday.—Thulin. Weather fine and bright. Reveille 6 a.m. Prepared for inspection by C.R.A. to-day. Sgt. J. A. Maclean rejoined the Battery from School of Signalling at Dunstable, England.

14th NOVEMBER.—Thursday.—Reveille 6 a.m. Weather fine and bright. Inspected by C.R.A. to-day.

15th NOVEMBER.—Friday.—Reveille 6 a.m. Weather fine and bright. Attached to First Division to-day. Daily rum issue officially cancelled. Commemoration of King Albert's birthday. Party of thirty men marched to Thulin Church at 10.30 a.m. Officer in charge of Party, Mr. Stanton. Major Aland, i/c 14th Brigade Party. The four Brigade Trumpeters sounded Reveille twice and Flourish twice. Three calls in church and one outside.

1918.

16th NOVEMBER.—Saturday.—Thulin. Reveille 6 a.m. Weather fine and bright. Nothing unusual occurred.

17th NOVEMBER.—Sunday.—Thulin. Reveille 6 a.m. Weather fine and bright. Lieut. V. J. Borland and Lieut. T. Sheard together with nineteen Other Ranks, were taken on strength to-day, consequent on the disbanding of the 5th Canadian Divisional Trench Mortar Brigade.

18th NOVEMBER.—Monday.—Thulin. Reveille 6 a.m. Weather fine and bright.

19th NOVEMBER.—Tuesday.—Moved from Thulin to Cambron St. Vincent. Reveille 12.15 a.m. Moved off at 3.30 a.m. Reached destination about 2 p.m. Weather damp, foggy and very cold. Inspected by O.C. 3rd Inf. Brigade, 1st Canadian Division *en route*.

20th NOVEMBER.—Wednesday.—Stayed at Cambron St. Vincent. Reveille at 6.30 a.m. Cleaned harness and vehicles to-day. Half holiday. Weather damp, misty and cold.

21st NOVEMBER.—Thursday.—Moved from Cambron St. Vincent to Braine le Comte. Reveille at 4 a.m. Filed out at 6.30 a.m. Reached destination at 1 p.m. Weather misty and cold. Made good time on march. Inspected by General MacDonnell of the 1st Canadian Division *en route*, who took the salute at Saigine. Cleaned harness and vehicles on arrival. Billets for all ranks in main street. Stables in factory and gun park in yard.

22nd NOVEMBER.—Friday.—Braine le Comte. Reveille 6.30 a.m. Cleaning harness and vehicles in forenoon. Half holiday in the afternoon. Weather fine but cold.

1918.

23rd NOVEMBER.—Saturday.—Braine le Comte. Reveille 6.15 a.m. Cleaning harness and vehicles in forenoon. Afternoon, holiday for drivers with clean harness, and gunners. Orders received for move on following day. Weather fine and bright; chilly.

24th NOVEMBER.—Sunday.—Reveille 4.30 a.m.; fall in 5 a.m.; breakfast 5.45 a.m. Filed out 7.30 a.m.; marched from Braine le Comte to Loupoigne. Horses in school yard. Men billeted in school. Officers' Mess and quarters in house next door. The Mayor of the village refused to sign Billeting Certificate, saying, "We don't want pay from our liberators."

25th NOVEMBER.—Monday.—Reveille 6.30 a.m. Cleaning harness and vehicles in forenoon. Left Loupoigne to-day for Villers la Ville. Filed out at 1 p.m. and reached destination at 5 p.m. General MacDonnell took the salute *en route.*

26th NOVEMBER.—Tuesday.—Villers la Ville. Reveille 6.30 a.m. Cleaning harness and vehicles in forenoon. Half-holiday in afternoon. Weather dark and damp. Parties from the Battery visited ruins of the Abbey.

27th NOVEMBER.—Wednesday.—Villers la Ville.—Reveille 4 a.m. Moved off at 7 a.m. Arrived at Cognelle about 5.30 p.m. Billets in lofts. Left Section and "G" Sub-section horses in stables, remainder on lines. Office in large chateau, occupied by French "evacuees." Weather wet and dark.

28th NOVEMBER.—Thursday.—Chateau grounds at Cognelle. Reveille at 6 a.m. Moved off at 9 a.m. for Hingeon. Arrived at 7 p.m. Horses in stables and billets in houses. Wet and dark.

1918.

29th NOVEMBER.—Friday.—Hingeon. Reveille 6 a.m. Moved off at 9.15 a.m. Arrived Sur-le-Mez at 2 p.m. Horses on picket lines and billets in houses. Dark and warmer.

30th NOVEMBER.—Saturday.—Reveille at 6 a.m. Moved off for Andenelles at 9 a.m. Arrived at 1 p.m.

1st DECEMBER.—Sunday.—Andenelles. Stayed in Andenelles all day to-day, as neither rations nor forage arrived. Harness cleaning and fatigues.

2nd DECEMBER.—Monday.—Andenelles. Reveille at 4 a.m. Order to move cancelled while trumpet was being sounded. A second Reveille was sounded at 6.30 a.m. The rations having arrived, the Battery moved off at 9 a.m. and marched to Bois-en-Bossu, arriving there about 5 p.m.

3rd DECEMBER.—Tuesday.—Bois-en-Bossu. Reveille at 6.30 a.m. Parade at 9 a.m. for inspection. Received orders to move, and moved at 10.15 a.m. The day was fine. We reached Verlaine about 3 p.m.—a little village perched on the side of a very steep hill. The horse lines are in the open, the gun park in a field outside the village, and the Officers and men are billeted in houses in the village.

4th DECEMBER.—Wednesday.—Verlaine. Reveille at 6 a.m. Moved off at 8 a.m. The day was a very poor one—cold, and with a heavy Scotch mist falling. We halted for dinner at the side of the road. After dinner the mist turned to a fairly heavy rain, and we had a rather dismal march to Chauveherd, arriving in the dark about 5 p.m. All horses, except fourteen, are in stables. The guns are parked in a field opposite the cookhouse. Officers and men are billeted in houses. The billets are not so good as we often have had on this march. The arrangements for rationing the men and horses on this move to Germany are very unsatisfactory.

1918.

5th DECEMBER.—Thursday.—Chauveherd.   Reveille at 6 a.m. Nothing very special.   Time spent in cleaning up the harness and vehicles.   The weather a decided improvement on yesterday.   Day was fine, with quite a number of periods of sunshine.

6th DECEMBER.—Friday.—Reville at 5 a.m.   Moved off at 7.40 and marched to Arbrefontaine, arriving there about 1 p.m. The weather is quite fine to-day, and there has been a good deal of sunshine on the trip.   We finally got clear to-day of the succession of deep valleys through which we have been travelling for the past four or five days.

7th DECEMBER.—Saturday.—Arbrefontaine.—Reveille at 4.15 a.m. Breakfast at 5.15 a.m.   Moved off at 7 a.m.   Marched to Recht.   Inspected *en route* by General Thacker. The day was fairly fine, but overcast.   Personnel billeted in houses through the village ; horses partly in stables and partly on lines alongside the gun park.   Between Arbrefontaine and Recht we crossed the frontier and entered Germany.   The frontier was indicated by two black-and-white posts and a sign-post.   The absence of any evidence of animosity of the Germans among whom we now are is nothing short of amazing. Outwardly they are most friendly and hospitable.

8th DECEMBER.—Sunday.—Recht.   Reveille at 5 a.m.   Marched at 8 a.m. to Krinkett.   The roads were heavy and bad towards the end of the march.   A number of the horses were under cover at night.   The billets for the men were only **fair.**

9th DECEMBER.—Monday.—Krinkett.   Reveille at 5.30 a.m. Marched at 8.30 to Weisin.   Arrived there about 4 p.m.   The roads for most of the march were very poor, and a slight fall of rain made matters worse.   The weather was only fair.   A fog descended about 9 a.m., turning to a slight rain, and then clearing up.   Horses are all in the open to-night.   Billets for the men are very poor and crowded. We were inspected *en route* by General MacDonnell, Commanding the 1st Canadian Division.   We were advised officially that Lieut. A. G. Virtue has been awarded the M.C., and the following men awarded the M.M. :—Sgt. Ward Brian Williams, Cpl. George Gustave Neher, Bdr. Edgar Lawrence Sprunt and Bdr. David Baillie Moffat.

1918.

10th DECEMBER.—Tuesday.—Weisin.   Reveille at 6 a.m.   Moved
off at 9 a.m. and marched to Commern.   The day was a
good one, and our route lay over much better roads than
yesterday.   The horses are picketed in the open on lines
formed by the vehicles.   The men are billeted in houses
through the town.   An issue of tobacco and cigarettes
to-day (the usual weekly issue delayed) relieved a serious
condition of stringency in the "smokes" line.

11th DECEMBER.—Wednesday.—Commern.   Reveille at 4.45 a.m.
Moved off at 7.30 a.m. to Weilerwist.   The roads were good
and the weather fine.

12th DECEMBER.—Thursday.—Weilerwist.   Reveille at 4.30 a.m.
Marched at 7.15 a.m. to outskirts of Cologne.   Weather was
only fair.   During the latter part of the journey it rained
on us.   Reached our destination at noon.   Billets in a barracks here, in which the 60th Battery is also quartered.
We marched over very good roads to-day.   A large amount
of Canadian parcel mail reached us this evening.

13th DECEMBER.—Friday.—Cologne Barracks.   Reveille at 5 a.m.
Moved off about 8.45 a.m. to march through the City of
Cologne.   The day was a very poor one, heavy rain falling
from early morning, and what might have been a really
fine show was rather spoiled by the weather.   Considerable
interest was displayed by the civilians in the parade, and
each street corner had a small group of spectators standing
under umbrellas.   Our route lay across the New Bridge
over the Rhine, onto which the head of the column marched
about 10.10 a.m.   The Brigade was inspected on the bridge
by Sir H. Plumer, Commanding 2nd Army, of which we
at present form a part.   Before starting, Captain C. King
(who is at present in charge of the Battery, in the absence
of Major Greene) inspected the Battery and awarded a prize
of 50 francs to Dvr. G. V. H. Clayton and one of 25 francs
to Gnr. J. S. Hughes for the best and second best team and
harness.   Our new billets are at Vingst.   Officers and men
are billeted in houses through the town, some of the Right
and Centre Sections being in a cinema theatre.   The Left
Section and "G" Sub. are in a school-house.   Both the
cinema and school were formerly occupied by German
troops, and there are quite decent "double deck" bunks
in them.

1918.

14th DECEMBER.—Saturday.—Reveille at 6.30 a.m. Inspection Parade 9 a.m. The morning was spent in cleaning harness and vehicles, the afternoon being a half-holiday. Major E. A. Greene rejoined the Battery to-day, having been absent since 24th October, when he left in order to proceed on leave to the United Kingdom. He was taken to hospital suffering from "Spanish 'flu" before he was able to embark. During this march the Battery has been complimented on its appearance by every Inspecting Officer. After inspecting the Brigade, General MacDonnell said it was "the best artillery I have seen in France," and that the 18-pounder Batteries were all so good that he could not make a choice of best.

15th DECEMBER.—Sunday.—Still in Vingst. Reveille at 6.30 a.m. Bathing Parade at 8.30 a.m. Lieut. Virtue, M.C., reported back from hospital to-day. The German civilians are quiet, orderly and obliging.

16th DECEMBER.—Monday.—Vingst. Nothing very special. Lieut. F. M. Stanton reported back from Brigade for duty. Weather very good. Slight showers.

17th DECEMBER.—Tuesday.—Still at Vingst. Half-holiday in the afternoon. Weather very good, though slightly colder to-day.

18th DECEMBER.—Wednesday.—Still at Vingst. Nothing very special. The usual cleaning work done. A check over all equipment is being made, so that everything may be in good shape when the time comes to hand over, as we expect demobilisation orders soon.

19th DECEMBER.—Thursday.—Vingst. Reveille 6.30 a.m.

1918.

20th DECEMBER.—Friday.—Vingst. A Nominal Roll asked for, which is to show civilian occupation of all ranks, as well as their intended area of demobilisation. There are thirteen areas of demobilisation, of which London is the first and Calgary the 13th; the intermediate districts have as centres the largest town in that district.

21st DECEMBER.—Saturday.—Vingst. Reveille at 6.30 a.m. Nothing very special. A complete check-over of all equipment has now been called for.

22nd DECEMBER.—Sunday.—Vingst. Reveille at 6.30 a.m. Nothing very special. Weather showery.

23rd DECEMBER.—Monday.—Vingst. Reveille at 6.30 a.m. A start made to-day on the Education Scheme. Lectures delivered.

24th DECEMBER.—Tuesday.—Vingst. Reveille at 6.30 a.m. Further lectures delivered to-day in connection with the Education Scheme. Weather fair. Canadian parcel mail has been arriving in large quantities for the past week.

25th DECEMBER.—Wednesday.—CHRISTMAS DAY. Vingst. Reveille 6.30 a.m. A whole holiday as far as possible. The Men's Christmas Dinner was held at 5 p.m. Roast pork, potatoes, boiled cabbage, plum pudding, nuts, dates, oranges, etc. Plenty of cigarettes. Weather fairly cold. A slight flurry of snow during the night. We are experiencing very little sickness at present in the Battery. On the whole, the health of the men is really very good. So far, this time, the Spanish influenza epidemic has not worried us much.

26th DECEMBER.—Thursday.—Still at Vingst. Nothing special.

1918.

27th DECEMBER.—Friday.—Received word that we are to exchange billets, etc., with the 66th Battery to-morrow. In consequence the day was spent principally in preparation for the move. Received notification that Lieut. C. H. Locke has been awarded the M.C.

28th DECEMBER.—Saturday.—Reveille at 5 a.m., and moved off at 8 a.m. Marched to Immekeppel. The day was a very poor one; it rained on us nearly all the way. Everything is very scattered here. The Left Section is in one place, with its own cook-house, etc., and the Right and Centre Sections are in houses round the Railway Station of Obersteeg. The Officers' Mess, Q.M. Stores, and Orderly Room are about a thousand yards from the Right and Centre Sections, towards the Left Section. The Officers' Mess and Q.M. Stores are in a boot-lace factory, and the Orderly Room in a house a few yards away.

29th DECEMBER.—Sunday.—Another miserable, wet day. Church Parade at 5.45 p.m. Captain Latimer came out from Vingst to take it.

30th DECEMBER.—Monday.—The weather improved, and the day was fine. Major Greene went to Brigade and Captain King is now acting O.C. Battery, with Lieut. C. H. Locke acting as Captain. Lieut. F. M. Stanton went on leave to Paris.

31st DECEMBER.—Tuesday.—Weather fairly fine to-day. A request from 1st Canadian Divisional Artillery for two more copies of the Nominal Roll in connection with Demobilisation.

1919.

1st JANUARY.—Wednesday.—A whole holiday as far as possible. The day was very fine—a good omen for the coming year.

1919.

2nd JANUARY.—Thursday.—The leave is proceeding satisfactorily
    at present. With the exception of a few men in hospital,
    all men who came with us to France have now had leave.

3rd JANUARY.—Friday.—Further lectures to-day in connection
    with the Educational Scheme. Lieut. C. H. Locke took up
    The Returned Soldiers' Land Settlement Bill, and Lieut.
    A. G. Virtue lectured on Civil Liability and Contracts.

4th JANUARY.—Saturday.—The weather has been on its best
    behaviour for the last couple of days, in marked contrast
    to what it was on our arrival up here.

5th JANUARY.—Sunday.—Another good day. Captain Latimer
    came out from Brigade to hold Divine Service at 5.30 p.m.

6th JANUARY.—Monday.—Captain C. King proceeded on leave to
    United Kingdom to-day. The weather continues very fine

7th JANUARY.—Tuesday.—A fine day.

8th JANUARY.—Wednesday.—As no mail has arrived for several
    days, we sent after it to-day. It arrived in the evening;
    plenty of letters and parcels.

9th JANUARY.—Thursday.—Another fine day. Nothing special
    to record.

1919.

10th JANUARY.—Friday.—Weather still continues fine. We submitted an "Entraining State" to-day.

11th JANUARY.—Saturday.—Nothing very special. An inspection of the horses was held. A photographer visited us, and took some Sub-section groups.

12th JANUARY.—Sunday.—A sprinkling of snow this morning. A Bathing Parade during the morning. The Padre (Captain Latimer) held service at 2 p.m. in the Hotel alongside the Main Cookhouse. Lieut. Norton, of "A" Battery, 187th Brigade R.F.A., his batmen and two Bombardiers arrived as Advance Party for the relieving Battery.

13th JANUARY.—Monday.—Rather damp and foggy during the early part of the night. Our mail arrangements have been decidedly unsatisfactory, and it was decided to-day to send an N.C.O. and one man daily to Kalk to collect it. They will also carry the outgoing mail.

14th JANUARY.—Tuesday.—Nothing of very special importance. The weather to-day was damp and uncertain. Very little mail arrived. Not a single letter for anyone in the Battery

15th JANUARY.—Wednesday.—Lieut. C. H. Locke, M.C., left us this morning for Canada, having been granted the privilege of early demobilisation. Lieut. Locke came to this Battery during the latter part of January, 1917, when the 59th Battery (Winnipeg) was broken up. The Right Section of the 59th Battery came at the same time—when Batteries ceased to be four-gun and became six-gun. Lieut. A. G. Virtue, being Senior Officer present, assumes charge of the Battery as Acting O.C.

1919.

16th JANUARY.—Thursday.—As we move to-morrow to the Huy area (Belgium), the day is being spent in general "cleaning up" and preparation for the move. We turned over all ammunition—1,052 rounds ("A" 745, "AX" 307)—to the A/187 R.F.A.

17th JANUARY.—Friday.—Reveille at 4.30 a.m. Moved off at 7 a.m. and reached a former German artillery camp at 11 a.m. This place is not far from Wahn. Here we watered, fed, and had lunch. We marched through "The King's Forest" *en route*. Moved off again at 1.15 p.m. and reached Wahn Station at 2 p.m. Entrained here and pulled out at 4 p.m. We had 16 men and 28 horses from the 2nd Section, 5th C.D.A.C., and 4 men and 4 horses from the Divisional Train with us, making a total Entraining State as follows :—188 Officers and other ranks, 8 waggons G.S. (including 2 from D.A.C. and 2 from Div. Train), 6 guns and limbers, 14 ammunition waggons (including 2 from D.A.C.), 1 mess cart, 1 water cart, 23 riding horses, and 168 light and heavy draught horses (including 4 from Div. Train and 28 from D.A.C.). We re-crossed the Rhine at 4.35 p.m. The night became very cold, and as the train was not heated, we had a somewhat comfortless trip.

18th JANUARY.—Saturday.—After travelling all night, we arrived at Andenne (not far from Huy) about 5 a.m. Here we detrained, and, after breakfast, moved off at 8.30 a.m., marching to Seron, where we watered, fed, and had lunch. At about 2 p.m. we resumed our march and reached Folx-les-Caves about 4 p.m. The day was fine when we started, but turned bitterly cold as the day advanced. At first it rained and later snowed very heavily, both rain and snow being accompanied by a piercing wind. Some of our road lay across country devoid of any shelter whatever, and the morning generally was distinctly an unpleasant one. The afternoon was slightly better, as very little snow or rain fell. Lieut. Stanton reported back from leave to Paris, and left the Battery at once to assume the duties of Staff Captain at Headquarters, 3rd C.D.A. Gunner J. O. Kirkland accompanied him.

1919.

19th JANUARY.—Sunday.—A fine day. Nothing very special. A little Canadian mail arrived. Our billets are, for the most part, fairly decent, but everything is very much scattered. Brigade Headquarters is at Jauche, about 3 kilos distant.

20th JANUARY.—Monday.—The weather is good, but fairly cold. Coal is scarce here. A fairly respectable amount of Canadian mail arrived, but, judging from the dates of the letters, there appears to be a good deal still missing.

21st JANUARY.—Tuesday.—Cold and frosty to-day. Half-holiday. Football match between two of the Sub-sections. We collected all German money possible in the Battery and sent it down to Huy for exchange. Lieuts. Virtue and Borland rode to Orp-le-Grand on reconnaissance for better waggon lines.

22nd JANUARY.—Wednesday.—Fine, frosty day. Got the exchange for our German money this evening. The rate of exchange is : 1 mark equals 67 centimes.

23rd JANUARY.—Thursday. Left our lines in Folx-les-Caves this morning at 9.30 a.m. and marched to new lines in Orp-le-Grand, about six kilometres from the first-named place. The gun park and the stables are in a large brick factory adjoining the railway station, the Officers' mess in a large house between the station and the railway crossing, the Sergeants' mess in a house to the left of the station entrance, the Q.M. stores in an outbuilding of the factory, and the men's billets through the town. To-day we were called on to prepare another Nominal Roll, to accompany completed "questionnaire" cards, issued by the Department of Soldiers' Civil Re-establishment, Canada. The card omits one important question, viz., Has the soldier any definite promise of immediate employment on his return to Canada ? We have received word that the O.C. (Major E. A. Greene) has been awarded the D.S.O.

1919.

24th JANUARY.—Friday.—Got a considerable amount of work done in connection with the new "questionnaire" cards.

25th JANUARY.—Saturday.—Leave is now available for men to visit Brussels, Namur, Liege, and Louvain. Our first five men left this morning. We got paid to-day—the first time since about the middle of December. The weather keeps very cold, but is bright and dry.

26th JANUARY.—Sunday.—Flurries of snow off and on all day. Decidedly cold still. Church Parade in the Recreation Room at 10.15 a.m., followed by the Sacrament of the Lord's Supper.

27th JANUARY.—Monday.—A light fall of snow during the night. Weather sunny and milder in the afternoon. We played the 60th Battery at football this afternoon, and won 3—1.

28th JANUARY.—Tuesday.—Cold to-day. Leave to the United Kingdom has been suspended at present, as no transport is available. It is being used to return troops to the Old Country.

29th JANUARY.—Wednesday.—Quite cold again to-day. No mail reached us. There was a parade at 2 p.m. All present and correct.

30th JANUARY.—Thursday.—Very cold to-day. There is no sign of a thaw, and the roads are very slippery. A photographer arrived from Brussels, and we had a "mounted" photo taken of the Battery. Played the 60th Battery at football, the score being 0—0.

1919.

31st JANUARY.—Friday.—At 9.30 a.m., photo of Battery dismounted. Weather continues frosty, with white film of snow on ground.

1st FEBRUARY.—Saturday.—Usual Saturday morning inspection. Everything in good shape. Building an oven to roast meat, and a brick fireplace in men's messroom.

2nd FEBRUARY.—Sunday.—Church Parade in Recreation Room at 10.15 a.m. under Captain Latimer.

3rd FEBRUARY.—Monday.—Word was received that Captain King, who went on leave January 8th, is ill in hospital at Hastings, England.

4th FEBRUARY.—Tuesday.—A slight thaw during the day, but it became cold again during the evening. We were called on for another Nominal Roll in connection with demobilisation. The particulars called for are slightly fuller than those contained in the Roll submitted on 26th December, 1918.

5th FEBRUARY.—Wednesday.—It thawed a bit to-day, but started to snow again in the evening, and quite a little fell. Lieut. Green delivered a lecture this evening dealing with the Government's Scheme of Land Settlement and various articles of interest along Re-establishment lines.

6th FEBRUARY.—Thursday.—A good deal of snow fell last night, but it could hardly be called a heavy fall. A picture show, with some other items interspersed, organised by the Sergeants, was a great success.

1919.

7th FEBRUARY.—Friday.—A very cold day. Severe frost and a cloudless sky. Pay Parade in the morning. The A.D.V.S. visited us to-day and "classed" our horses for demobilisation purposes.

8th FEBRUARY.—Saturday.—A biting cold day. Bright sunshine. The Y.M.C.A. opened a Canteen in our Recreation Room to-day. There is evidently a tie-up in the Mail somewhere. We have not had a Canadian Mail, except a few letters, for over a month.

9th FEBRUARY.—Sunday.—Very cold again to-day. The Padre held Service in the Recreation Room at 2 p.m.

10th FEBRUARY.—Monday.—Lieut. A. G. Virtue proceeded on leave to Italy to-day, and Lieut. R. Wildgoose took over command of the Battery. We had some Canadian Mail in to-night, the first for quite a time.

11th FEBRUARY.—Tuesday.—Not quite so cold to-day, but still bright and clear. Lieut. R. Wildgoose received orders to-night to return to England for early demobilisation.

12th FEBRUARY.—Wednesday.—We got 52 horses handed over to us to look after for the present. They are some of the Canadian Cavalry horses that have been turned in. We hold them till the Belgian Government takes them over. Lieut. G. S. Raley reported back from Brigade.

13th FEBRUARY.—Thursday.—The weather during the last couple of days has been warmer, and the snow is slowly melting. Lieut. R. Wildgoose left us, *en route* to Canada, via England. Lieut. G. S. Raley took over command.

1919.

14th FEBRUARY.—Friday.—The weather is quite mild again to-day and the sky overcast. Quite a good Canadian letter mail arrived to-night. We turned in our Questionnaire Cards duly completed, as well as a Roll containing all the information on these Cards tabulated. Also an analysis of the number of men proceeding to each of the Dispersal Stations.

15th FEBRUARY.—Saturday.—Thawing all day to-day. Warmer. We were supplied with a schedule of sailings for the Canadian Corps. We sail about 21st April.

16th FEBRUARY.—Sunday.—Very mild again to-day. The Padre held service here at 2 p.m.

17th FEBRUARY.—Monday.—Orders received to hand over the 52 Cavalry Horses to the Belgian Government. The Party is to start on the 20th, the Billeting Party leaving on the 19th. All horses are to be branded before leaving. All horses are to be handed over in Brussels, and the trip will take two days. All the snow has now melted, and the ground round the stables is a sea of mud.

18th FEBRUARY.—Tuesday.—We received orders last night to turn in an amended Roll showing any men who wished to take advantage of what amounts to a "stop over" privilege in Eastern Canada. The scheme is that such men will be demobilised in the East and provided with a free warrant to their final destination, good for one month. Roll was turned in before 6 p.m.

19th FEBRUARY.—Wednesday.—Our Advance Billeting Party, consisting of A./Bdr. McCauley and Gnr. Ragotte, left this morning, riding two of the horses to be turned over. The balance of the horses were branded to-day. The weather continues very mild, and the mud is as plentiful as ever.

1919.

20th FEBRUARY.—Thursday.—Sgt. Wray, accompanied by 33 Other Ranks, left for Brussels with 50 horses to be turned over to the Belgian Government. The Party was supplied with three G.S. Waggons. Included in the party were one cook and one shoeing smith. Horses to be turned over on 22nd.

21st FEBRUARY.—Friday.—Nothing of particular importance. Weather uncertain.

22nd FEBRUARY.—Saturday.—Weather rainy at times, and lots of mud everywhere.

23rd FEBRUARY.—Sunday.—Church Parade at 2 p.m.

24th FEBRUARY.—Monday.—Owing to the danger of "Flu." the Cinema and our Recreation Room were closed this evening. A fairly large Canadian Mail in.

25th FEBRUARY.—Tuesday.—Nothing special. Weather very mild and inclined to rain.

26th FEBRUARY.—Wednesday.—Nothing special.

27th FEBRUARY.—Thursday.—Lieut. V. J. Borland went on leave to-day.

28th FEBRUARY.—Friday.—Lieut. A. G. Virtue reported back from leave to-day. There is very little of interest these days. Beyond the necessary work with the horses there is very little to do.

1919.

1st MARCH.—Saturday.—A very fine mild day. We played the 60th Battery at Indoor Baseball and won. Gnr. G. H. Selvage and Dvr. F. G. King captured two escaped German prisoners of War this afternoon, near Ramillies. The capture was a very smart piece of work. The Fritzies had come quite a long way and were walking along the railway when they were seen. Doctor Seaton gave a very interesting exhibition of Conjuring this afternoon. It was greatly appreciated, and was a very enjoyable break in the monotony.

2nd MARCH.—Sunday.—The Padre held service at 2 p.m. to-day. It was in the open air, as all inside Services, Cinemas, etc., are banned at present on account of the "Flu." So far we have got off lightly as regards this epidemic, and any cases that we have had have not been serious ones. A little Canadian mail arrived to-night, but a really big mail (with "beaucoup" letters for everyone) seems to be a thing of the past.

3rd MARCH.—Monday.—The weather was poor to-day. Very rainy at times. Doctor Seaton gave another entertainment in the Recreation Room to-night.

4th MARCH.—Tuesday.—The weather is rainy again to-day, and there is no lack of mud. We were requested to move the horses from the factory buildings, as the proprietors wish to start the plant operating again. There is likely to be a good demand for the product in France—BRICKS.

RETROSPECT.

THE story of our experiences as a Battery would hardly be complete without an expression of some of the thoughts that have been common to all, or without a reference to the impressions which a glance backwards leaves upon us.

Our existence as a Battery can be roughly divided into five periods, viz :—The period of training in Canada from April 3rd, 1916, to September 11th, 1916; the period of training and waiting for orders in England, which continued until August 20th, 1917; the period of "Trench" Warfare in France on the Lens, Loos, La Bassée and Oppy Fronts until August 1st, 1918; the greatest period of all—the "Open" Warfare period which began with the Amiens "Show" on August 8th and continued as an unbroken series of advances until the Canadians reached Mons on November 11th, 1918; and finally, the period from November 11th, 1918, to in which we waited impatiently for the orders to return to Canada.

Probably one of the first questions a member of the Battery will ask himself is, "Did we fulfil our functions as a Battery, and are we satisfied with our work?" On the whole, we may feel that we can honestly answer ourselves in the affirmative. So far as we know, the Infantry whom we from time to time supported, including the 1st, 3rd, and 4th Canadian Divisions, the 51st British (Scottish) Division, and several other Imperial Divisions, were satisfied with our work, and on many different occasions they were kind enough to express their satisfaction in letters to the Officers Commanding our Division, Brigade, and Battery respectively.

Probably another question we shall ask is, "What of our losses?" In the whole period of nearly fifteen months our losses were six killed and twenty wounded. The great majority of the wounded are already fit again, or nearly so. On a score of occasions we have remarked, "Well, there is certainly a horseshoe around this Battery!" But in our most serious thoughts we have many times felt a deep gratitude to a merciful Providence for what seemed to us wonderful escapes from inevitable catastrophe. When we consider the number of occasions on which the gunners served their guns with the "odd shell" going everywhere but into our detachments, the countless journeys by night and by day made by the drivers over roads constantly harassed by the Hun, the daily trips by signallers and look-out parties to and from O.P.'s in areas which were recognised as unhealthy, and the score of other ways in which everyone was more or less continually exposed—when we consider all these things, we are inclined to pause in amazement at the smallness of our casualty list, and to feel a deep sense of gratitude that it is so. Probably it is not realised that to a very great degree casualties in war, according to our experience, vary in inverse ratio to the precautions taken. Over and again the minute care taken in the selection of a gun position; the anxious study of this route and that for our movements and ammunition supply; the reasoned solutions of the score of problems of time and place which constantly come up—all these things on many occasions proved the difference between safety and heavy losses.

Of our comrades who made the supreme sacrifice, we can only say that, to a man, they were what true soldiers should be; their courage and gallantry were an example to us all, and they will always live in our memories as generous comrades and true men. To their loved ones who sorrow for them every man in the Battery gives his sympathy, and his assurance that no man in France did his duty more nobly than they.

When we think of our part in the war we naturally think of the hardships we have had to bear—Army discipline itself, "bully and biscuits and Maconochie," bedrooms varying all the way from smelly, damp cellars and "crummy" dug-outs and wet shell-holes, to nothing at all; semi-annual baths, and various other things which are best left unsung. And yet on the whole we believe almost everyone of us will admit to himself that it was not so bad after all, and certainly not so bad as we had anticipated. Human nature being what it is, some of us will doubtless shortly essay the innocuous remark, "Oh, for the good old days at ——," and be mobbed as a result.

During our service in France we saw the supremacy of the air definitely taken from the Germans and placed safely in the hands of our own airmen. Sometimes it seemed that we were getting the worst of it, but taken in all 1918 was decidedly "our" year in the air.

The absence of crime in our Battery has been marked. The few cases that did arise were almost without exception of a trivial character, and we can regard our sheet as a clear one.

No retrospect would be just or fair that did not pay a tribute to our cooks. Despite the cries of "That —— Maconochie again!" and "How will you have your eggs this morning?" we have realised that our cooks have done work of the highest excellence, and when the men of this Battery went without a meal (which after all was practically never) it was because no cooks on earth could have provided one.

Our "Paper War" was ably conducted, and our proud boast is that for every memo. Brigade sent in we shot two out, while the unutterable abuse that was heaped upon that seldom-seen object called "The Army System" would have done credit to a worthier cause.

We feel compelled also to refer to the work of the man upon whom our water supply depended—No. 524072 Private Ainsley, E. L. (C.A.M.C.). He was the Gunga Din of the 61st Battery—happily without a tragic ending. Rain or shine, hot or cold, gas or bombs, frost or mud—the old Water Cart with its stalwart nags, and with Ainsley tramping behind, rolled and bumped up to the Battery position and back again in its own particular unconcerned fashion. In the whole period of our service the old Water Cart never failed us, and every man in the Battery feels nothing but admiration for this branch of our service and the man responsible for it.

Our experience is that a six-gun battery requires four G.S. Waggons, and not merely one. Also we are "all for" motor-traction in the next war.

This leads us to think of our horses. One, Charles Westley, a gunner in our Battery in the early days, summed up the horse situation in a masterly way. When chided by one of the officers for kicking a horse which had gently embraced him about the neck, instead of "speaking to the horse," Westley said, "I-I-I'll s-s-speak to him, sir, when I g-get him a-alone." And it may be said that the men of our Battery were on speaking terms with our horses, but desired no closer acquaintanceship. But in spite of the weariness of grooming, we admit that our horses played their part nobly. They never gave in, and they never failed to get our guns and ammunition to its appointed place. In fact, we have a fine bunch of horses, and they played the game as well as any of the richly-bedecked chargers of bygone wars.

And when anyone speaks of harness-cleaning, please refer him to the 61st, who have a special emery-cloth and brasso treatment for everyone found suffering from this deadly disease after the war

We would be ungrateful to pass over the work of the Y.M.C.A. without an expression of our thanks to it. The Y.M.C.A. has proved a very great friend to us in France, and without it our life would have been a much more unpleasant one. The "Y" shared its profits with us, and we received nearly 4,000 francs in all, which was expended for extra messing, Christmas dinners, and other benefits.

Taking a broad view of our whole experience of war as a Battery, we have had good fortune throughout; we have been able to take the hard things cheerfully; but it will be the greatest day of our lives when we are once more in Canada and out of uniform and done with the war.

ROLL OF HONOUR.

LIEUT. C. E. M. RICHER.—Wounded 2nd September, 1918, while the Battery was moving forward through Vis-en-Artois. Died 3rd September, 1918.

SGT. (ACTING B.S.M.) WALLAS, W. A.—Wounded by the same shell as Lieut Richer (who was walking with him). Died the same day.

CPL. CLAPSTONE, L.—Wounded by Area fire while the Battery was in position in front of Vis-en-Artois on 2nd September, 1918. Died the same day.

BBDR. WOOD, J. T.—Killed in action instantly while the Battery was answering an S.O.S. call on the morning of 5th April, 1918.

GNR. McSPADDEN, W. H.—Wounded by a stray shell on 21st October, 1918. Died the following day.

GNR. GRANT, R.—Accidentally killed while demolishing a house, 22nd October, 1917.

During the period 22/8/17 to 11/11/18, we have had twelve men wounded and evacuated to England, as follows :--

GNR. BARNES, R. D.—6/9/17.—Splinter in back.

DVR. ROBERTS, W.—3/10/17.—Splinter from "Woolly Bear" in hand.

GNR. WILSON, C. S.—18/1/18.—Splinter from "Woolly Bear" in finger.

GNR. NICHOL, H. L.—5/4/18.—Splinters in head, shoulder, back, hand and arm.

BBDR. CHAMBERS, W. G.—2/6/18.—Splinter from "Woolly Bear" in hip.

DVR. OWENS, G.—2/9/18.—Splinter in arm.

GNR. KINSEY, C. V.—2/9/18.—Splinter in head.

A./BBDR. LYONS, A. H.—3/9/18.—Splinter in leg.

GNR. COLCHESTER, W. M.—6/9/18.—Splinter in back.

CPL. McNEIL, J. E.—27/9/18.—Severely wounded in arm.

GNR. WALDIE, J. C.—10/10/18.—Wounded by a piece of bomb that exploded while Battery was on the line of march.

SIG. McTEER, K. G.—5/11/18.—Wounded in the side from harassing fire.

We also have had eight men wounded and returned to us, whose wounds were not serious enough to necessitate evacuation to England :—

GNR. CLIFFORD, A.—5/4/18.—Splinter in back.

GNR. RICHBELL, E.—5/4/18.—Splinter in leg.

SIG. FRY, J. C.—9/6/18.—Splinter in hand.

SGT. WILLIAMS, W. B.—26/8/18.—Wounded in the groin by the accidental explosion of a bomb of some kind.

GNR. MILNE, C. F.—26/8/18.—Wounded in the arm at the same time.

GNR. SELVAGE, G. H.—30/8/18.—Splinter in the back from a bomb dropped by an enemy airman.

DVR. HEATHERTON, R.—1/9/18.—Splinter from a "Woolly Bear" in back.

DVR. ST. OURS, L.—29/10/18.—Splinter through shoulder.

HONOURS AND AWARDS.

DISTINGUISHED SERVICE ORDER.
    Major E. A. Greene.

MILITARY CROSS.
    Capt. C. King, Lieut. C. H. Locke, Lieut. A. G. Virtue, Lieut. R. H. Babbage.

MENTIONED IN DESPATCHES.
    Major E. A. Greene, Lieut. G. S. Raley.

    NOTE.—Lieut. R. Wildgoose was awarded the D.C.M. prior to joining the Battery, and was entitled to wear the 1914-1915 Star.

MILITARY MEDAL.
    Sgt. C. F. Wray, Sgt. W. B. Williams, Cpl. G. G. Neher, Bbdr. D. B. Moffat, Bbdr. E. L. Sprunt, Gnr. R. Watson, Dvr. J. H. Ross.

MERITORIOUS SERVICE MEDAL.
    Gnr. E. C. Turcotte.

    NOTE.—Dvr. J. Grassick was entitled to wear the 1914-1915 Star.

LIST OF REINFORCEMENTS.

Major E. A. Greene.
Capt. C. King.
Lieut. F. M. Stanton.
Lieut. C. G. Quinn.
Lieut. R. Wildgoose (D.C.M.).
Lieut. C. E. M. Richer.
331781 Gnr. Bland, G. H.
264158 Dvr. Bates, W. C.
311934 Dvr. Bowman, A. E.
333872 Dvr. Barnard, W.
345075 Dvr. Campbell, J. D.
1251446 Dvr. Congdon, K. G.
1258126 Dvr. Currie, F. R.
1251965 Dvr. Dickson, H. B.
339783 Dvr. Delcourt, C.
742884 Dvr. Fulford, J. E.
327926 Dvr. Gannon, J. S.
1251146 Gnr. George, E. H.
442082 Gnr. Gibberd, F. E.
467259 Gnr. Gorrie, W. E.
273975 Dvr. Higgins, R.
311419 Gnr. Hollinger, J.
345969 Dvr. Hollister, G. R.
340338 Dvr. Holley, J. J.
342369 Dvr. Hollingworth, H.
331821 Sig. Horspool, G.
340340 Dvr. Hyde, F. C.
2557454 Dvr. Jackson, A. F.
2522378 Dvr. Jackson, W. M.
341297 Gnr. Kinsey, C. V.
343222 Gnr. Ker, M. F.
1250861 Gnr. Kathan, S. G.
1251435 Dvr. Kanneman, E.
770107 Gnr. Kirkland, J. O.
343232 Dvr. Love, C. W.
3055390 Dvr. Lameront,
        M. L. H.
782253 Bbdr. Moffat, D. B.
339969 Gnr. Moore, C. D.

706123 Dvr. Marley, T. H.
2522399 Gnr. Moore, T. R. L.
336151 Gnr. Murchie, H. A.
340545 Dvr. Morgan, J.
344025 Gnr. Murray, L. A.
316943 Gnr. McElwaine,
        W. A.
829821 Gnr. McKeon, A. P.
340005 Gnr. McCalla, G. C.
92841 Sig. MacNeill, W. C.
339768 Gnr. McBryde, W. D.
1260736 Dvr. McLean, C. R.
2044139 Dvr. McGimpsey, T.
1251203 Dvr. McCleary,
        D. E.
339769 Dvr. McGilvray, M.
273811 Dvr. O'Brien, G. H.
343046 Dvr. Ogilvy, C.
334286 Dvr. Putnam, C. M.
320918 Dvr. Rogers, J.
1260685 Dvr. Roche, H. E.
1251368 Dvr. Robertson,
        W. H.
1262733 Dvr. Sanford, A. A.
307704 Dvr. Simpson, C. F.
349361 Sig. Sykes, C. W.
343162 Dvr. Street, H.
348592 Dvr. St. Ours, L.
338831 Dvr. Thompson,
        R. L. R.
4923 Dvr. Williams, A. S.
338341 Gnr. Weichel, C. J.
341334 Dvr. White, B. M.
338307 Dvr. Wilson, H. R.
334575 Dvr. Worth, W. J.
1251436 Dvr. Young, J. C.
        ATTACHED.
228336 Vet.-Sgt. Forsyth,
        N. S.

LIST OF OFFICERS & OTHER RANKS
STRUCK OFF STRENGTH
(Other than Killed or Wounded)

Between 22nd August, 1917, and 11th November, 1918.

Major Browne, G. S.—28/11/18.—To Hospital, sick.

Capt. Collinson, C. H.—16/10/18.—To 32nd Battery, C.F.A., as Major.

Lieut. Oliver, A. G.—11/12/17.—To Brigade Headquarters.

Lieut. Babbage, R. H.—4/11/18.—To England, sick.

Lieut. Quinn, C. G.—2/4/18.—To 58th Battery, C.F.A.

327960 Dvr. Allen, R.—1/11/18.—To England, sick.

331875 Gnr. Barrett, W.—8/9/18.—To England, accidentally injured.

331894 Cpl. Sad. Bridgeman, J. N.—22/10/18.—To England, sick.

1260388 Gnr. Burrows, B.—12/9/18.—To England, for R.A.F. Course.

327980 Gnr. Clifford, A.—7/9/18.—To England, sick.

331924 Dvr. Crowe, J. P.—6/6/18.—To England, accidentally injured.

445 Dvr. Clarke, J. S.—28/7/18.—To England, sick.

331890 Sig. Dawson, L. L.—22/4/18.—To England, sick.

331809 Dvr. Donnan, J. W.—6/7/18.—Transferred to 5th C.D.A.C.

327958 Sgt. Evans, A. E.—30/4/17.—To England, sick.

534439 Dvr. Fraser, D. S.—29/7/18.—To England, for R.A.F. Course.

332894 Dvr. Gardner, A. N.—5/10/17.—To England, sick.

1260305 Dvr. Griffin, O. R.—17/6/18.—Transferred to Can. Labour Pool.

331897 Gnr. Hamilton, J. J.—26/10/18.—To England, sick.

1260368 Gnr. Hamilton, R.—28/11/17.—To England, sick.

116502 F./Sgt. Hardy, M.—20/10/18.—To England, sick.

331921 Gnr. Headrick, W. A.—29/7/18.—To England, for R.A.F. Course.

331820 Gnr. Henderson, J. D.—28/12/17.—To England, sick.

331821 Sig. Horspool, G.—24/12/17.—To England, sick.

331823 Dvr. Hudson, W. E.—20/10/18.—To England, sick.

311419 Dvr. Hollinger, J.—7/10/18.—To England, classified "U.S.F."

231040 Gnr. King, G.—27/5/18.—To England, accidentally injured.

327860 Sgt. Link, N.—8/8/18.—To England, for R.A.F. Course.

339969 Gnr. Moore, C. D.—10/1/18.—To England, sick.

336151 Gnr. Murchie, H. A.—24/10/18.—To England, accidentally injured.

331906 Sig. McTeer, D.—25/10/18.—To England, sick.

316943 Gnr. McElwain, W. A.—24/3/18.—Transferred to 5th C.D.T.M. Bde.

340005 Gnr. McCalla, G. C.—21/1/18.—Transferred to Bde. Headquarters.

331845 Dvr. Page, W.—11/12/17.—Transferred to Bde. Headquarters.

331861 Dvr. Paris, R. J. C.—1/11/18.—Transferred to 32nd Battery, C.F.A.

231019 Gnr. Protheroe, E. J. T.—Aug./1917.—Transferred to H.Q., 5th C.D.A.
327928 A./Bbdr. Pull, J.—-13/12/17.—To England, sick.
327945 Dvr. Reynolds, L. M.—8/11/18.—To England, sick.
320918 Dvr. Rogers, J.—13/8/18.—Transferred to Can. Labour Pool.
116389 Gnr. Smart, E. H.—7/11/18.—To England, sick.
1260412 Dvr. Smith, J. M.—1/11/18.—Transferred to 32nd Battery. C.F.A.
1262733 Dvr. Sanford, A. A.—6/7/18.—Transferred to 5th C.D.A.C.
331855 Gnr. Turcotte, J. A.—12/9/18.—To England, for R.A.F. Course.
331910 A./Bbdr. White, H. A.—3/6/18.—To England, sick.
338341 Gnr. Weichel, C. J.—6/10/18.—To England, sick.

ATTACHED.

324917 V./Sgt. Clark, G. A.—8/5/18.—To England, for R.A.F. Course.
327893 B.S.M. Walker.—13/6/18.—Promoted Regimental Sgt.-Major.

NOMINAL ROLL

As at 11th November, 1918.

Major Greene, E. A. (D.S.O.).
Capt. King, C. (M.C.).
Lieut. Locke, C. H. (M.C.).
Lieut. Virtue, A. G. (M.C.).
Lieut. Raley, G. S.
Lieut. Stanton, F. M.
Lieut. Wildgoose, R. (D.C.M.).
331903 Gnr. Armstrong, A. C.
327949 Gnr. Armstrong, H. J.
331928 Sgt. Baillie, J. B.
327910 Gnr. Barnard, G. A.
333872 Dvr. Barnard, W.
331870 Sig. Bass, W. H.
264158 Dvr. Bates, W. C.
332924 Gnr. Belford, J. J.
327904 Sgt. Bellingham, A. B.
331781 Gnr. Bland, G. H.
1260350 Dvr. Blogg, J. W.
311934 Dvr. Bowman, A. E.
327957 Gnr. Bowman, H.
332834 Bbdr. Bradley, J.
332835 Dvr. Bridges, W.
331609 Dvr. Browning, F. E.
331889 Gnr. Brunsdale, N. C.
331913 Bbdr. Bryant, C. A.

327913 Dvr. Birrell, J.
345075 Dvr. Campbell, J. D.
331914 Sig. Carr, C. B.
327887 Gnr. Carter, A. C.
327890 Bbdr. Champion, D. A.
327882 Dvr. Cheetham, J. C. H.
331807 Cpl. Christianson, T.
687185 S/S. Clark, J. G.
1260352 Dvr. Clayton, G. V. H.
331805 A/Bbdr. Collier, W. W.
1251446 Dvr. Congdon, K. G.
331922 Dvr. Connolly, T.
332896 Gnr. Cook, J.
331806 Dvr. Coupland, A.
1258126 Dvr. Currie, F. R.
331876 Gnr. Currier, F.
327916 Dvr. Davey, W. H.
331808 Gnr. Davies, A.
339783 Dvr. Delcourt, C.
332817 Gnr. de Sausmarez, C. A. W.
1251965 Dvr. Dickson, H. B.

331882 Sgt. Douglass, L. V.
331810 Gnr. Dow, R.
161233 Dvr. Downie, J.
327874 Dvr. Ellis, E.
327966 A/Bbdr. Emerson,
          R. R.
331811 Sig. Faunch,
          E. J. H.
706149 Dvr. Ferguson, G.
706411 Gnr. Ferguson, R.
327952 Gnr. Field, W. M.
327869 Sig. Finnsson, F.
331813 Dvr. Foreman, J.
331884 Sig. Fry, J. C.
742844 Dvr. Fulford, J. E.
327926 Dvr. Gannon, J. S.
331815 A/Bbdr. Gaught, H.
1251146 Gnr. George, E. H.
327851 Gnr. Gerrard, W. G.
442082 Gnr. Gibberd, F. E.
467259 Gnr. Gorrie, W. E.
327885 Whlr. Goswell, E. A.
331816 Cpl.-S/S. Graham, G.
331900 Dvr. Grant, J.
 77952 Dvr. Grassick, J.
331868 Dvr. Griffiths, S.
327855 Gnr. Hargrave, C.
331898 Dvr. Harrison, T. W.
331879 Dvr. Hayward, V. M.
331770 Dvr. Heatherton, R.
332827 Dvr. Hinchcliffe, W.
273975 Dvr. Higgins, R.
345969 Dvr. Hollister, G. R.
340338 Dvr. Holley, J. J.
342369 Dvr. Hollingworth, H.
331821 Sig. Horspool, G.
327895 A/Bbdr. Howden,
          C. B.
331919 Dvr. Hudson, T. A.
331822 Bbdr. Hudson, W.
331824 Gnr. Hughes, J. S.
216999 Dvr. Hume, J. McN.
340340 Dvr. Hyde, F. C.
331871 Sig. Ironside, G. L.
2557454 Dvr. Jackson, A. F.
2522378 Dvr. Jackson, W. M.
331909 A/Bbdr. Johnston,
          H. O.
1260413 Gnr. Jones, A.
216460 Gnr. Jones, C.
331892 Sdl. Jones, D. O.
332840 Dvr. Jones, W.
331829 Gnr. Jones, W. H.
1251435 Dvr. Kanneman, E.

1250861 Dvr. Kathan, S. G.
1260369 Dvr. Kelway, S.
231085 Bbdr. Kenwood, F. H.
343222 Gnr. Ker, M. F.
327932 Dvr. Kilgour, J. W.
331830 Dvr. King, F. G.
327969 Gnr. King, F. R.
770107 Dvr. Kirkland, J. O.
3055390 Dvr. Lameront,
          M. L. H.
331831 A/Cpl. Leys, R. A.
343232 Dvr. Love, C. W.
331839 B.Q.M.S. Manning,
          T. H.
706123 Dvr. Marley, T. H.
 13901 Gnr. Marshall, S.
331841 Gnr. Martin, B. B.
331881 Dvr. Mason, H. R.
331887 Cpl. Massey, G. A.
332891 Gnr. Mattin, F.
327857 Dvr. Mayers, F. T.
913018 Dvr. Medlicott, G. G.
231188 Gnr. Millar, J.
331891 Bbdr. Miller, D.
331923 Dvr. Mills, I.
332892 Gnr. Milne, C. F.
782253 Bbdr. Moffat, D. B.
339969 Dvr. Moore, C. D.
2522399 Gnr. Moore, T. R. L.
340545 Dvr. Morgan, J.
1260416 Dvr. Morry, D. W.
344025 Gnr. Murray, L. A.
332914 Gnr. McBrady, D. J.
339768 Gnr. McBryde, W. D.
331907 A/Bbdr. McCauley,
          H. W.
1251203 Dvr. McCleary, D. E.
327853 Dvr. McCreath, S.
331834 Dvr. McDonald, J.
327867 Dvr. McFerran, R. J.
339769 Dvr. McGilvray, M.
2044139 Dvr. McGimpsey, T.
829821 Gnr. McKeown, A. P.
331911 S/S. Mackie, A. J.
331877 Dvr. Mackie, D.
331880 Sig. McKinnon, M. M.
1260736 Dvr. McLean, C. R.
116182 Sgt. McLean, J. A.
331838 Dvr. McLean, R. G.
 92841 Sig. McNeill, W. C.
327959 Dvr. McQueen, J.
331912 Sig. McTeer, K. G.
327898 Cpl. Neher, G. G.
273811 Dvr. O'Brien, G. H.

99

343046 Dvr. Ogilvy, C.
706561 Dvr. Parkes, F. C.
327894 Bbdr. Patterson, G.
1260403 Bbdr. Pellow, F.
327954 Dvr. Pennycook, W. A.
332887 Dvr. Piper, P. J.
331847 Gnr. Powell, A.
334286 Dvr. Putman, C. M.
327879 Gnr. Ragotte, G.
331849 Gnr. Rennison, G. G.
327935 Gnr. Richbell, E.
1260436 Gnr. Ritchie, R. A.
1251368 Dvr. Robertson, W. H.
1260685 Dvr. Roche, H. E.
180127 Dvr. Rogers, J. E. M.
1260391 Dvr. Ross, J. H.
331866 Gnr. Roy, J. L.
331886 Dvr. Samson, F. S.
327940 Dvr. Sangster, L. A.
327906 Dvr. Scott, C. W.
331927 B.S.M. Scougall, G. H.
307704 Dvr. Simpson, C. F.
216459 Gnr. Selvage, G. H.
231633 Gnr. Smith, A. J.
331852 Ftr. Smith, P
327918 Bbdr. Speers, K. E.
331895 Bbdr. Sprunt, E. L.
883686 Gnr. Srigley, R. J.
216844 Dvr. Steen, J.
391853 Gnr. Stewart, J.
343162 Dvr. Street, H.
808646 Tptr. Stringer,
  E. C. O.
348592 Dvr. St. Ours, L.

736497 Gnr. Sutherland, A.
349361 Sig. Sykes, C. W.
327953 Gnr. Tanner, A. B. W.
331854 Dvr. Thomas, W.
338831 Dvr. Thompson,
  R. L. R.
116419 Sig. Thursby, S. F.
331908 Gnr. Turcotte, E. C.
116251 Sig. Vallance, D.
116436 Gnr. Walden, A.
331862 Gnr. Wallwork, J. H.
331905 A/Bbdr. Walshe,
  R. F.
231167 Gnr. Watson, R.
331901 Sgt. Weatherley,
  G. W.
341334 Dvr. White, B. M.
4923 Dvr. Williams, A. S.
327862 Sgt. Williams, W. B.
338807 Dvr. Wilson, H. R.
327866 Dvr. Wilson, D. W.
331860 Dvr. Wolstencroft, J.
331863 Cpl. Woods, J. E.
334575 Dvr. Worth, W. J.
331859 Sgt. Wrav, C. F.
910159 Gnr. Wright, J. M.
327891 Cpl. Young, A. J. W.
1251436 Dvr. Young, J. C.

ATTACHED.

524072 Pte. Ainsley, E. L.
  (C.A.M.C.)
228336 Vet.-Sgt. Forsyth,
  N. S. (C.A.V.C.)

www.ingramcontent.com/pod-product-compliance
Lightning Source LLC
Chambersburg PA
CBHW032001060426
42446CB00040B/748